Insights to Excellence 1996

Also available from ASQC Quality Press

The Reward and Recognition Process in Total Quality Management
Stephen B. Knouse

Staffing the New Workplace: Selecting and Promoting for Quality Improvement
Ronald B. Morgan and Jack E. Smith

Integrating Reengineering with Total Quality
Joseph N. Kelada

Making Training Work: How to Achieve Bottom-Line Results and Lasting Success
Berton H. Gunter

Avoiding the Pitfalls of Total Quality
Charles C. Poirier and Steven J. Tokarz

The Change Agents' Handbook: A Survival Guide for Quality Improvement Champions
David W. Hutton

Benchmarking: The Search for Industry Best Practices That Lead to Superior Performance
Robert C. Camp

Business Process Benchmarking: Finding and Implementing Best Practices
Robert C. Camp

LearnerFirst™ Benchmarking 1.0 software
with Dr. H. James Harrington, International Quality Advisor—Ernst & Young, L.L.P.

LearnerFirst™ Process Management software
with Tennessee Associates International

To request a complimentary catalog of publications, call 800-248-1946.

Insights to Excellence 1996

An Inside Look at the 1996 Baldrige Award Criteria

Mark L. Blazey

ASQC Quality Press
Milwaukee, Wisconsin

Insights to Excellence 1996: An Inside Look at the 1996 Baldrige Award Criteria
Mark L. Blazey

Library of Congress Cataloging-in-Publication Data
Blazey, Mark L.
    Insights to excellence 1996: an inside look at the 1996
  Baldrige Award criteria / Mark L. Blazey
      p. cm.
    Includes index.
    ISBN 0-87389-412-X (alk. paper)
    1. Total quality management—Awards—United States.
  2. Benchmarking (management)—United States. 3. Malcolm Baldrige
  National Quality Award.   I. Title.
  HD62.15.B58   1996
  658.5'62'07973—dc20   96-21967
                                  CIP

10 9 8 7 6 5 4 3 2 1

ISBN 0-87389-412-X

Acquisitions Editor: Roger Holloway
Project Editor: Jeanne W. Bohn

ASQC Mission: To facilitate continuous improvement and increase customer satisfaction by identifying, communicating, and promoting the use of quality principles, concepts, and technologies; and thereby be recognized throughout the world as the leading authority on, and champion for, quality.

Attention: Schools and Corporations
ASQC Quality Press books, audiotapes, videotapes, and software are available at quantity discounts with bulk purchases for business, educational, or instructional use. For information, please contact ASQC Quality Press at 800-248-1946, or write to ASQC Quality Press, P.O. Box 3005, Milwaukee, WI 53201-3005.

For a free copy of the ASQC Quality Press Publications Catalog, including ASQC membership information, call 800-248-1946.

Printed in the United States of America

 Printed on acid-free paper

Quality Press
611 East Wisconsin Avenue
Milwaukee, Wisconsin 53202

This book is dedicated to the memory of my father, Everett Blazey Jr., and to my mother, Ann Marrer Blazey—two people who taught me the value of continuous improvement.

Contents

vii

Preface

A substantial portion of my recent professional life has been spent helping people become quality award examiners. These people come from all types of organizations and from all levels within those organizations. Participants include corporate quality directors, state organization chiefs, small business owners, heads of hospitals, and school superintendents—to name a few. This book was originally developed for them. It was used as a teaching text to guide their decisions and deliberations as they provided feedback to organizations that documented their continuous improvement efforts using Baldrige Award–type management systems. Many examiners who used this text asked me to publish it in a stand-alone format. They wanted to use it to help their own organizations, customers, and suppliers guide and assess their continuous improvement efforts.

These two groups of readers—examiners of quality systems and leaders of high performing organizations—can gain a competitive edge by understanding not only the parts of a high performance management system, but how these parts connect and align. My goal for this book is that readers will understand fully what each area of the quality system means for organizations and find the synergy within the seven major parts of the system: leadership, information and analysis, strategic planning, human resources development and management, process management, business results, and customer focus and satisfaction.

Corporate and education leaders have reported that this book has been valuable as a step-by-step approach to help identify and put in place continuous-improvement systems. As this progresses, improvement efforts in one area will lead to improvements in other areas. This process is similar to experiences we have all encountered as we carry out home improvement: Improve one area and many other areas needing improvement become apparent. This book will help identify areas that need immediate improvements as well as areas that are less urgent but, nevertheless, vitally linked to overall improvement.

Acknowledgments

I acknowledge the support and guidance of Curt Reimann of the Malcolm Baldrige National Quality Award office; the typing assistance of Stephanie Madalena; the design and layout by Enterprise Design and Publishing; and the substantive contributions of Karen Davison and Jeff Martin of the New York Excelsior Award, John A. Pieno Jr. and Dione Geiger of the Florida Sterling Council, Beverly Centini of the Pennsylvania Quality Leadership Awards, and Mary Gamble of Hellmuth, Obata, and Kassabaum (HOK) architects.

Mark L. Blazey

Introduction

This introductory section includes some suggestions about how to start down the path to systematic organizational improvement. The introductory section also provides ideas on transition planning, training, and, finally, lessons learned from those who chose paths that led nowhere or proved fatal despite their best efforts.

Connections and Linkages

A popular children's activity, connect-the-dots, helps kids understand that, when properly connected, apparently random dots create a meaningful picture. In many ways, the 7 categories, 24 items, and 52 areas to address in the Baldrige Award criteria are like the dots that must be connected to reveal a meaningful picture. With no paths to make the web, or join the dots, human resources is isolated from strategic planning, information and analysis is isolated from process management, and overall improvement efforts do not yield robust results. This book describes these linkages for and between each item. The exciting part about having them identified is that you can look for these linkages in your own organization and, if they don't exist, start building them.

Transition Strategies

Putting high performance management systems in place is a major commitment that will not happen quickly. At the beginning, you will need a transition strategy to get you across the bridge from management by opinion or intuition to more data-driven management. The next section of this introduction describes one approach that has worked for many organizations in various sectors: creating a performance improvement council.

Council Structure

Identify a top-level executive leadership group of 6 to 10 members. (Each member over that number will seem to double the complexity of issues and make decision making much more cumbersome.) The executive leadership group could send a message to the entire organization by naming the group the Performance Improvement Council—reinforcing the importance of continuous performance improvement to the future success of the organization.

The Performance Improvement Council becomes the primary policy-making body for the organization. It spawns other Performance Improvement Councils at the lower levels to push practices and policies to every employee in the organization as well as involving customers and suppliers. The structure permeates the organization as members of the Performance Improvement Council become area leaders for major improvement efforts and sponsors for several process or continuous-improvement task teams throughout the organization.

Council Membership

Selecting members for the Performance Improvement Council should be done carefully. Each member should be essential for the success of the operation and together they must be sufficient for success. The most important member is the senior leader. This person must participate actively—demonstrating the kind of leadership that all should emulate. Other members would have leadership for broad areas of the organization such as human resources, operations planning, customers, and data systems.

Performance Improvement Council Training and Planning

The Performance Improvement Council should be extremely knowledgeable about high performance management systems. If not, as is usually the case, Performance Improvement Council members should be among the first in the organization to receive training in continuous-improvement tools and processes. However, that training should be carried out in the context of planning—that is, learn tools, then use them to plan the quality implementation, practices, and policies.

The Performance Improvement Council should

- Develop an integrated, continuous-improvement strategic performance improvement and business plan.

- Create the web (communication plan and infrastructure) to transmit quality policies throughout the organization.

- Define the roles of employees, including new recognition and reward structures to cause needed behavior change.

- Develop a master training plan. Involve team representatives in planning so they can receive skills close to when they are needed. Define what is provided to whom, when.

- Launch quality improvement projects that will produce both short- and long-term successes. Projects would be defined by the Performance Improvement Council consistent with the strategic plan and could include important administrative processes such as career development, performance measurement, and diversity, as well as improving operational products and services in the line areas.

- Develop a plan to communicate the new successes of the organization.

Through this approach, quality-improvement management processes are defined by the top leadership of the organization. Ownership and commitment to action are enhanced through this planning process, reducing the barriers to implementation and change.

The Critical Skills

A uniform message, set of skills, and constancy of purpose are critical to success. The courses that make up core quality training should provide all employees with the knowledge and skills on which to build an organization that continually gets better.

- Team building and communications, as well as effective meeting management provide a starting place for effective teamwork, problem solving, and employee involvement.

- Another important core skill involves using a common process to define customer requirements accurately, determining our ability to meet those requirements, and measuring our success and determining the extent to which our customers—internal and external—are satisfied.

- When a problem arises, employees must be able to define the problem correctly, isolate the root causes, generate and select the best solution to eliminate the root causes, and implement the best solution.

- It is also important to make decisions based on facts, not intuition or feelings. Therefore, understanding tools that improve the ability to analyze work processes and performance data is important. With these tools, work processes can be analyzed and vastly improved. Reducing unnecessary steps in work processes, increasing control, and reducing cycle time are powerful ways to improve quality and reduce cost simultaneously.

- More advanced courses in benchmarking, in work process improvement and reengineering supplier partnerships and certification, in role models for managers, in integrating strategic planning and quality planning, and in customer satisfaction will help managers and employees expand their quality thrust across the entire organization.

Practical Insights

Twenty years ago the fierce global competition that inspired the quality movement was felt primarily by major manufacturers. Today, all sectors are under intense pressure to "be the best or be history." The demand for quality reaches all corners of our economy, from manufacturing and service industries to professional services, education, health care, and government. All of these segments have contributed valuable lessons to the quality movement and have played an important part in our recovery from the economic slump caused by poor quality service and products of the 1970s. Relying on the Baldrige Award model, we will share some of the insights and lessons learned from quality leaders.

Leadership

Great Leaders Are Great Communicators Who Lead by Example

One characteristic of a high performance organization is outstanding performance results. How does an organization achieve such results? How does it become world-class? While no scientific studies have been able to document a single road that leads to such success, we have found unanimous agreement on the critical and fundamental role of leadership. There is not one example of an organization or unit within an organization achieving profound improvement without the personal and active involvement of its top leadership. Top leadership in these organizations creates a powerful vision that focuses and energizes the work force. Everyone is pulling together toward the same goals. Frequently an inspired vision is the catalyst that overcomes the organizational status quo.

Great leaders are great communicators. They identify clear objectives and a game plan for their organization to succeed in its mission. They assign accountabilities, ensure that employees have the tools and skills required, and create an environment that rewards teamwork and data-driven improvement. They also practice what they preach, serving as a role model for continuous improvement and fact-based decision making, and pushing authority and accountability to the lowest possible levels.

Lessons Learned About Leadership

Minimize the use of the word *quality*. Too often, when skilled, hard-working, dedicated employees are told by leadership, "We are going to start a quality effort," they conclude that their leaders believe they have not been working hard enough. The work force hears an unintended message, "We have to do this because we are not good." They frequently retort with, "We already do quality work." The registered professional often exacerbates the problem by trying to explain that customers (or the profession) define quality, not the employees. These messages confuse the work force. In short, the use of the word *quality* can create an unintended barrier of mistrust and negativism that leadership must overcome before even starting on the road to higher performance.

As an alternative, leaders should create an environment that inspires the work force to improve continually the way they work—to seek higher performance levels and reduce the work that does not add value or optimize performance. Most readily agree that there is always room for improvement. The use of the word *quality* can also open leadership to challenges as to what definition of quality the organization should use. This leads to the second lesson learned.

Leadership will have to overcome two organizational tendencies—to reject any quality model or theory "not invented here" and to think that there are many equally valid quality models. Quality differs from a decision tree or problem-solving model where there are many acceptable alternatives. The Baldrige Award model—and the many national, state, and company assessment systems that are based on it—is widely accepted as the definition of a standard for excellence in organizational performance worldwide. Its criteria provide validated, leading-edge practices for managing an organization. Nearly a decade of extraordinary business results shown by Baldrige Award–based winners and numerous state-level, Baldrige Award–based award winners have helped convince those willing to learn and listen.

To be effective, leaders must understand the Baldrige Award model and communicate to the work force and leadership system their intention to use that model for assessment and improvement. Without clear leadership commitment to the comprehensive Baldrige Award model, resources may be spent chasing facts or narrowly focused, isolated strategies such as reengineering, quality circles, and ISO 9000 certification, to name a few. Without clear leadership there will be many "hikers" walking around but no marked trails for them to follow. Once leaders understand the system and realize it is their responsibility to share the knowledge and mark the trails clearly, performance optimization is attainable. This brings us to our third leadership lesson learned.

A significant portion of leadership's time, as much as 60 percent to 80 percent, should be spent in visible Baldrige Award–related leadership activities, such as goal setting, planning, reviewing performance, recognizing and rewarding high performance, and spending time understanding and communicating with customers and suppliers. Leadership's perspective in goal setting, planning, and reviewing performance must look to the inside from the outside. Looking at the organization through the critical eyes of external customers, suppliers, and other stakeholders is a vital perspective. The primary role of the effective senior leader is not to manage internal operations, but rather to be visionary and focus the organization on satisfying customers.

Information and Analysis

Data-Driven Management and Avoiding Contephobia

The high performance organization collects, manages, and analyzes data and information to drive excellence and improve its overall performance. Using data and information as strategic weapons, leaders constantly compare their organization constantly to competitors, similar service providers, and world-class organizations.

While we tend to think of data and measurement as objective and hard, there is often a softer by-product of measurement. That by-product is the basic human emotion of fear. This perspective on data and measurement leads to our first lesson learned about information and analysis. We must recognize and manage human fear as we practice data-driven management.

This fear can be found in two types of people. The first are those who have a simple fear of numbers—those who hated mathematics in school and probably stretch their quantitative capabilities to balance their checkbooks. These individuals are lost in numerical discussions, so when asked to measure or when presented with data, they become fearful and resistant. Their reactions and anger can actually undermine improvement efforts.

The second type of individual, while understanding numbers, realizes numbers can impose higher levels of accountability. The fear of accountability, *contephobia* (from 14th-century Latin "to count," modified by the French "to account") is based on the fear of real performance failure that might be revealed by numbers or, more often, an overall fear of the unknown that will drive important decisions. Power structures can shift when decisions are data driven.

Fearful individuals can undermine effective data-driven management systems. In managing this fear, leadership must believe and communicate through behavior that a number is not inherently right or wrong. It is important that leaders at all levels demonstrate that system and process improvement, not individuals, are the focus of performance improvement.

A seasoned, high performance organization will collect data on competitors and similar providers and benchmark itself against world-class leaders. Some individuals may not be capable of seeing the benefit of using process-performance information. This type of data is known as generic benchmarking data. The focus is on identifying, learning from, and adopting best practices or methods from similar processes regardless of industry or product similarity. Adopting the best practices of other organizations has driven quantum leap improvements, providing great opportunities for break-through improvements.

Lesson number two, therefore, tells us an organization that has difficulty developing analogies between itself and dissimilar businesses is not ready to benchmark and is not likely to be able to optimize its own results.

Strategic Planning

Strategic Planning = Quality Improvement Planning

The quality organization's strategic plan is its improvement plan. Developing a separate quality plan is very likely to create a nonintegrated, and hence short-lived, quality or systematic performance improvement effort. Therefore, leaders should not write a separate quality plan. Rather, concentrate on two or three critical improvement goals in your strategic plan, such as improving customer satisfaction and reducing errors or cycle time.

The most critical lesson learned when it comes to your strategic improvement plan is: Do not rest until you are certain every person in your organization knows your strategic plan and can tell you how he or she contributes to achieving the plan's goals and objectives. Remember the trail-blazing analogy? Don't let the hikers onto the trails until they all know where they are going, what they have to do to get there, and how to measure progress so they know they are going in the right direction and are maintaining satisfactory progress.

A standard technique used by examiners on quality assessment visits is to meet with the chief executive officer to gain an understanding of the personal vision and plan for the organization. The examiner will then interview the receptionist and many others at all levels and ask them to explain the organization's vision plan and their role in achieving the plan. In quality-based, high performance organizations, the examiner gets the same story from people at all levels of the organization. Even more, the examiner gets a sense that the vision and plan are real and attainable. Ensure that your strategic plan does not merely rest in a prominent position on the bookshelves of top managers. Ensure that it is used to drive actions and is understood by most workers. If all these actions are not taken, people may work hard but are likely to pull in several directions. It is critical to get everyone in the work force pulling in the same direction.

Human Resource Development and Management

The Big Challenge Is Trust

The quality, high performance organization develops and realizes the full potential of its employees. The organization that is committed to human resource excellence maintains an environment that builds *trust*. Trust is essential for employee participation, empowerment, and personal and professional growth, as well as high organizational performance.

The first human resource lesson is perhaps the most critical one. That is, you must revise—overhaul, if necessary—your recognition, compensation, promotion, and feedback systems to support high performance work systems. If leaders demonstrate all the right quality leadership behaviors, yet continue to recognize fire-fighting individual performance, offer pay and bonuses tied to traditional bottom-line results, and promote individuals who do not represent high performance role models, those leaders should not be surprised if their improvement effort is short lived.

Critical to human resource excellence are communication and skill development. Training should not take the place of organization leaders communicating the vision, mission, and goals. Training can help reinforce messages, but it is a mistake to have trainers assume the responsibility of communicating organizational goals.

A second human resource lesson learned relates to training. Understand that training is not a panacea. Training does not do well in a vacuum. Resources spent to "train the troops" must be part of an overall strategic plan. If training is not part of such a plan, consider spending your money on a memorable holiday party. Above and beyond all other considerations, training can never, never take the place of clear, measurable organizational goals and a management strategy to target, reinforce, and use the training skills.

Timing is critical. Work force skill training should not come first. Many organizations rush out and train their entire work force only to find themselves having to retrain months or years later. Training rollouts should occur only after the organization has in place quality systems described in categories 1, 2, 3, and part of 4. Involve key trainees in planning the training so important skills are delivered just-in-time for them to use on the job.

Skill development requires training and management support to strengthen skills on the job. New technology has increased training flexibility, so all knowledge does not have to be transferred in a classroom setting. Consider many options, including training when planning how best to update skills. After initial skill building occurs, and the transformation to a learning culture is complete, some high performing organizations emphasize organizational learning where employees take charge of their own learning using training courses as one avenue for skills upgrade.

Two final human resource excellence lessons have to do with empowerment. Empowerment without a sense of direction is chaos, not quality. First, managers who empower employees before communicating and testing that a sense of direction has been fully understood will find they are managing chaos not quality.

Second, not everyone wants to be empowered, and such employees represent barriers to high performance. While there may be individuals who truly seek to avoid responsibility for making improvements, claiming "that's management's job," these individuals do not last long in a quality organization. Team members who want to help the organization thrive do not permit it.

The bigger reason for individuals failing to "take the empowerment and run with it" is management's mixed messages. In short, management must convince employees that managers really do believe their people know their own processes best and can improve them. Absolutely consistent leadership is required to help workers overcome legitimate fear of traditional management practices used so often in the past to control and punish.

Revising your reward system is one of the most critical things you can do for the success of a quality initiative. However, remember that getting employees to believe you really trust them to improve their own process is the most difficult.

Process Management

Keep Process Owners Involved

Process management is the continuous improvement of processes required to meet customer requirements and deliver quality products and services. Virtually every high performance organization identifies key processes and manages them to ensure that current customer requirements are met consistently, and quality and operational performance are continuously improved.

The first lesson learned here has to do with what we call the visibility of processes. Many processes are concrete and, therefore, visible. When a process is invisible, however, as so many are in the service sector, it cannot be assumed that everyone will see the organization as a collection of processes. The simple exercise of drawing a process flow diagram among people involved in an invisible process can be a struggle but, also, a revelation. With no vantage point from which to see work as a process, many people never think of themselves engaged in a process. Some even deny it. The fact that all work—visible and invisible—is a part of a process must be understood throughout the organization before you can begin to manage and improve key processes.

Once this is understood, a second process management lesson comes to light. Process owners are the best ones to improve their processes. They must be present on process improvement teams. Teams are often made up of cross-discipline, cross-functional, multilevel people. It is easy to lose sight of the process owner—the person who has expert knowledge of the process and who should be accountable for long-term improvement to that process. In an effort to ensure that all of its process improvement teams were cross-functional and multilevel, one organization enlisted volunteers to sit on the teams. A marketing process improvement team ended up with no marketers on it and a group of frustrated support and technical staff who knew nothing about marketing.

The third process management lesson learned involves an issue mentioned earlier. When examining internal processes and assessing the quality of products and services, it is easy to forget that quality and continuous improvement are strategic issues. Process analysis is tactical. There is a tendency when looking at internal processes to lose sight of external requirements. Organizations often succeed at making their processes better, faster, and cheaper for them, but not necessarily for the benefit of their customers. When analyzing internal processes, someone must stubbornly play the role of advocate for the external customer's perspective. Avoid wasting resources on process improvements that do not benefit customers, workers, or the financial performance of your organization.

Business Results

Encourage Activities That Lead to Desired Business Results

Results fall into four broad categories: Product and service quality, operational and support performance, human resource excellence, and supplier performance.

Product and service quality results report on key measures of the product or service itself that allow an organization to predict whether customers are likely to be satisfied—without asking them. For example, one of the nation's most successful and fastest growing coffee shops knows from its customers that a "good cup of coffee" is "hot," "has a good taste, not too bitter," and "has a rich aroma." The measures are temperature, pH (acidity), and time lapsed between brewing and serving. With these measures, employees can predict, before they serve it, whether their customers are likely to be satisfied with the coffee. If the measures you select do not correlate with, and predict, customer satisfaction, you probably have the wrong measures or not enough measures.

Operational and service results pertain to measures of internal effectiveness that may not be of immediate interest to customers, such as cycle time (how long it takes to brew a pot of coffee), waste (how many cups you have to pour out because the coffee has set too long), and payroll accuracy (which may be of concern to some affected workers, to name a few.) Ultimately, improving work processes can result in reduced cost, rework, waste, scrap, and other factors that affect your bottom line—whether profit-driven or budget-driven. Accordingly, your customers are indirectly affected. To stay in business, to remain competitive, or to meet increased performance demands with fewer resources, your organization will be required to improve processes that affect operational and support service results.

Supplier quality performance can significantly affect your operating effectiveness and customer satisfaction. To the extent you depend on suppliers, your organization must ensure that its supplier performance improves—otherwise you will be hurt by their waste, errors, inefficiency, and rework. An organization that tolerates poor supplier quality risks its own business.

Customer Focus and Satisfaction

Customers Expect Solutions to Problems They Don't Know They Have

The high performance organization systematically determines its customers' short-term and long-term service and product requirements. It builds relationships with customers and continuously gains information to improve its service and products. The smart organization determines the satisfaction and loyalty of its customers, compares itself to its competitors, and continuously strives to improve its satisfaction and loyalty levels.

As the organization becomes more and more systematic in determining customer needs, it becomes evident that there is high variation in customer needs. The more sophisticated your measurement system, the more variation will become apparent. An important first lesson is to segment your customers and build relationships with them. More and more customers are looking for service providers to define their unique needs for them and respond to those unique needs. In short, customers are expecting solutions to problems they, the customer, have not even realized. Organizations that make it easy for customers to complain, and handle those complaints at the first point of contact, find that customer loyalty and satisfaction will increase.

Lesson two has to do with educating your organization's leadership in the fundamentals of customer satisfaction and customer satisfaction research models before you begin collecting customer satisfaction data. Failure to do this may affect the usefulness of the data as a strategic tool. At the very least, it will make the development of data collection instruments a long, misunderstood effort, creating rework and unnecessary cost.

Do not expect everyone to welcome customer feedback. Time and time again, the organization that is most resistant to surveying customers, conducting focus groups, and making it easy for customers to complain is the same organization that does not have everyday contact handling systems, response time standards, or trained, empowered front-line employees. Their front-line employees are not ready to acknowledge customer feedback nor are they capable of assuming responsibility to solve customer problems.

This is the organization whose customers, when given the chance to provide feedback, announce they will not bother to complain anymore; they simply will no longer do business with the organization.

Finally, no one feedback tool is intended to stand alone. A mail-based survey does not take the place of one-on-one interviews. Focus groups do not replace surveys. The high performance organization uses multiple listening posts and trains front-line employees to collect customer feedback and improve those listening posts. In the high performance organization, for example, an accounts receivable system is viewed as a listening post.

Do not lose sight of the fact that the best customer feedback method, whether it be a survey, focus group, or one-on-one interview, is only a tool. Make sure the data those tools gather are actionable, and use those data to improve your strategic planning and operating processes.

Insights to Excellence

The Malcolm Baldrige National Quality Award criteria and scoring guide-lines present a powerful diagnostic instrument to help leaders identify organizational strengths and key areas for improvement.

Effective management systems are not simple. They consist of an intricate series of complex relationships between management and labor, customers, and suppliers. The best organizations improve work processes continually. They measure every key facet of business activity and closely monitor organizational performance.

Unfortunately, because of the complexity of modern management systems, the criteria used to examine them are also complex and difficult to understand. *Insights to Excellence 1996* seeks to help quality examiners and organization-improvement practitioners understand clearly the 1996 Baldrige Award criteria, and the linkages and relationships between the items.

Five types of information are provided for each of the 24 items that comprise the criteria.

- *The actual language of each item*

- *A "plain English" explanation of the essence of the item*

- *A summary of the requirements of the item in flowchart form*

- *The key linkages between each item and the other items*

- *Examples of effective practices*

Overall, *Insights to Excellence 1996* will strengthen your understanding of the criteria and provide perception in analyzing your organization and applying for the award.

Baldrige Award Categories and Point Values

Examination Categories/Items	Maximum Points
1.0 Leadership (90 points)	
1.1 Senior Executive Leadership	45
1.2 Leadership System and Organization	25
1.3 Public Responsibility and Corporate Citizenship	20
2.0 Information and Analysis (75 points)	
2.1 Management of Information and Data	20
2.2 Competitive Comparisons and Benchmarking	15
2.3 Analysis and Use of Company-Level Data	40
3.0 Strategic Planning (55 points)	
3.1 Strategy Development	35
3.2 Strategy Deployment	20
4.0 Human Resource Development and Management (140 points)	
4.1 Human Resource Planning and Evaluation	20
4.2 High Performance Work Systems	45
4.3 Employee Education, Training, and Development	50
4.4 Employee Well-Being and Satisfaction	25
5.0 Process Management (140 points)	
5.1 Design and Introduction of Products and Services	40
5.2 Process Management: Product and Service Production and Delivery	40
5.3 Process Management: Support Services	30
5.4 Management of Supplier Performance	30
6.0 Business Results (250 points)	
6.1 Product and Service Quality Results	75
6.2 Company Operational and Financial Results	110
6.3 Human Resource Results	35
6.4 Supplier Performance Results	30
7.0 Customer Focus and Satisfaction (250 points)	
7.1 Customer and Market Knowledge	30
7.2 Customer Relationship Management	30
7.3 Customer Satisfaction Determination	30
7.4 Customer Satisfaction Results	160
Total Points	**1000**

The Award Criteria

The criteria's seven categories and 24 items focus on requirements that all businesses—especially those facing tough competitive challenges—need to understand thoroughly. The criteria address all aspects of competitive performance in an integrated and balanced way. This includes improvement of: customer- and market-related performance; productivity in the use of all assets; speed and flexibility; product and service quality; cost reduction; and overall financial performance.

The criteria address key business processes and results, and are designed for diagnosis and feedback. All criteria directly relate to improving business performance—nothing is included merely for purposes of an award.

The criteria do not call for specific practices or organizational structures, because there are many possible approaches. The best choices depend upon many factors, including your organization's type, size, strategy, and stage of development.

Benefits of Participation

Over the years, award applicants have reported numerous benefits. Commonly cited benefits are

- Responding to the criteria forces a realistic self-assessment that, when combined with the comprehensive feedback report received from the award's Board of Examiners, targets key gaps and priorities for improvement. The overall assessment also recognizes and reinforces organization strengths.

- The pace of performance improvement is accelerated.

- The knowledge gained from assessment and feedback teaches new and better ways to evaluate suppliers, customers, partners, and even competitors.

- Use of the award criteria in assessment leads to the integration and alignment of numerous activities, previously loosely connected. The assessment provides an effective means to measure progress and to focus everyone in the organization on the same goals.

- Use of the award criteria helps companies understand, select, and integrate appropriate management tools such as reengineering, ISO 9000, quality management, activity-based costing, just-in-time production, lean manufacturing, flexible manufacturing, benchmarking, and high performance work.

The award criteria and scoring system provide a clear perspective on the distinction between typical performance and world-class performance.

Dynamic Relationships

The criteria are divided into seven categories that reflect the major components of a quality management system.

The **driver**, or enabler, is leadership. Without effective, visible, personally committed leadership, the quality system will falter. Failure to implement high performance work systems is directly traceable to problems with leadership at all levels.

The **system** is described by the categories of Information and Analysis (which is the "brain center" of the system), Strategic Planning, Human Resource Development and Management, Process Management, and some processes in Customer Focus and Satisfaction. Information systems are at the heart of the work and decision making of the organization. Information and analysis are used by leaders and workers at all levels to manage and improve their own work processes, to plan, and to promote work force excellence.

Progress is **measured** through the factors described in the Business Results and Customer Focus and Satisfaction Results area. These include measures of product and service features that enable organizations to predict ultimate customer satisfaction; measures of work efficiency and effectiveness; measures of human resource excellence; and measures of supplier performance.

Finally, the **goals** of this continuous-improvement system are satisfied customers, market share, increased competitiveness, better product and service quality, operational and financial performance, supplier performance, human resource performance, asset productivity, and public responsibility. All parts are necessary for a world-class, high performance organization.

Dynamic Relationships

The goal of the Baldrige Award is to help organizations enhance competitiveness.

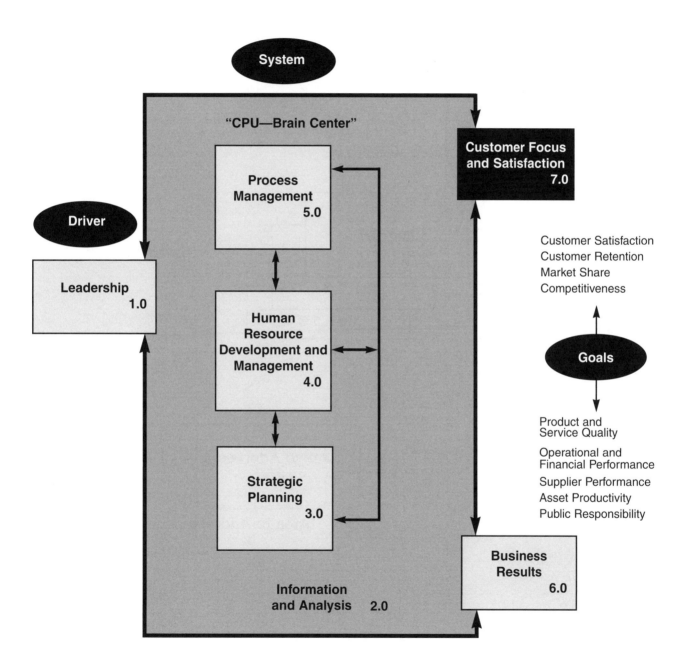

Each of the seven categories is made up of several items; each item contains one or more areas to address.

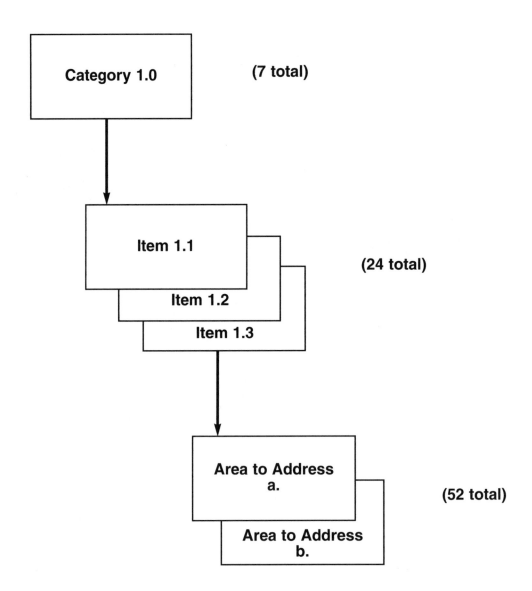

1.0 Leadership—90 Points

The Leadership category examines senior executives' personal leadership and involvement in creating and sustaining a customer focus, clear values and expectations, and a leadership system that promotes performance excellence. Also examined is how the values and expectations are integrated into the company's management system, including how the company addresses its public responsibilities and corporate citizenship.

1.1 Senior Executive Leadership (45 Points)

Describe senior executives' leadership and personal involvement in setting directions and in developing and maintaining an effective, performance-oriented leadership system.

Areas to Address:

a. How senior executives provide effective leadership and direction in building and improving company competitiveness, performance, and capabilities. Describe how senior executives: (1) create and maintain an effective leadership system based upon clear values and high expectations; (2) create future opportunity for the company and its stakeholders, set directions, and integrate performance excellence goals; and (3) review overall company performance, capabilities, and organization.

b. How senior executives evaluate and improve the company's leadership system, including their own leadership skills.

Notes:

(1) "Senior executives" means the applicant's highest-ranking official and executives reporting directly to that official.

(2) Values and expectations [1.1a(1)] should take into account needs and expectations of key stakeholders—customers, employees, stockholders, suppliers and partners, the community, and the public.

(3) Review of overall company performance is addressed in 1.2b. Responses to 1.1a(3) should focus on senior executives' roles in such reviews, and their use of the reviews to set expectations and develop leadership.

(4) Evaluations of the company's leadership system [1.1b] might include assessment of executives by peers, direct reports, and/or a board of directors. It might also include use of surveys of company employees.

This item is scored using the **approach/deployment** scoring guidelines. It addresses how the company's senior executives set strategic direction and build and maintain a leadership system conducive to high performance, individual development, and organizational learning. Executive leadership needs to consider all stakeholders—customers, employees, suppliers, partners, stockholders, the public, and the community.

Area 1.1a calls for information on the major aspects of leadership—creating values and expectations, setting direction, developing and maintaining an effective leadership system, and building company capabilities. Senior executives need to reflect these values, and the leadership system needs to include teamwork at the executive level.

Area 1.1b calls for information on how senior executives evaluate and improve the effectiveness of the company's organization and leadership system—including assessing and improving their own effectiveness as leaders. This aspect of leadership is crucial because of the fast pace of competition. A major target is to create organizations that are flexible and responsive— changing easily to adapt to new needs and opportunities. This area recognizes that both leadership and organization are crucial to high performance. Through their roles in strategy development and review of company performance, senior executives align leadership and the organization to changing opportunities and requirements.

1.1 Senior Executive Leadership

How senior executives provide leadership and become personally involved in setting direction and in developing and maintaining a leadership system for performance excellence

Building and Improving Performance

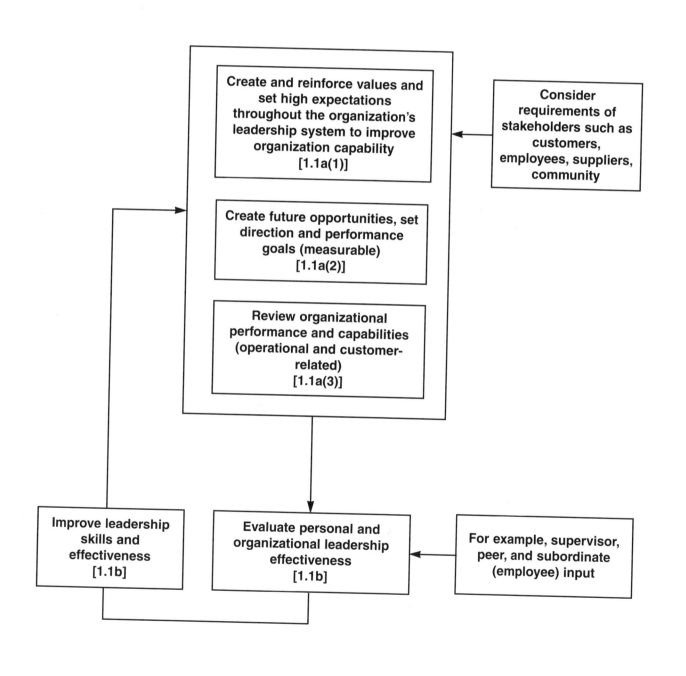

1.1 Senior Executive Leadership Item Linkages

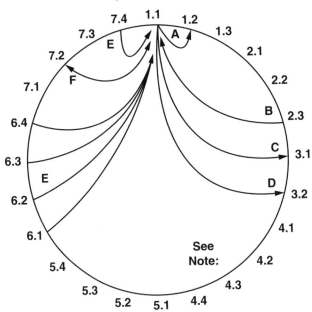

Item	Nature of Relationship
A	Senior executives [1.1] set, communicate, and cascade vision and quality values to managers throughout the organization [1.2]; they set performance expectations [1.1b] and review conformance to plans [1.2c]. Senior executives [1.1a] provide a role model for managers to focus on customers and high performance objectives; they provide mentoring and rewards and recognition to managers [1.2a].
B	Senior executives [1.1b(3)] use data collected for decisions regarding allocation of resources and priorities to serve customers better [2.3a(1)], improve operating effectiveness [2.3a(2)], competitive performance [2.3a(3)], and maximize financial returns [2.3b].
C	Senior executives [1.1b(2)] participate in strategic planning and work to improve the planning and plan deployment process [3.1].
D	Senior executives [1.1b(2)] approve the goals and measurements set forth in the plan [3.2b] and assist in deploying the plan throughout the organization [3.2a].
E	Senior executives monitor organizational performance [6.1, 6.2, 6.3, and 6.4] and customer satisfaction [7.4].
F	Senior executives [1.1b(1)] develop personal relationships with key customers, conduct visits, and consult with them [7.2]. Senior executives receive feedback from customers to aid in planning and decision making to keep the organization focused on serving the customer.

NOTE: Often, top executives become directly involved in human resource planning [4.1] and supporting high performance work teams [4.2], reward and recognition [4.3], and strengthening employee satisfaction and well-being [4.4]. More often, these activities are supported through the leadership system [1.2]. The relationship is described in that Item.

1.1 Senior Executive Leadership—Sample Effective Practices

A. Personal Involvement—Inspiring High Performance

- All executives are personally involved in performance improvement.
- The number of hours spent on quality and performance improvement activities occupies a significant portion of the executive's time.
- Executives carry out many visible activities (such as goal setting, planning, and recognition and reward of performance and process improvement).
- Executives regularly communicate quality values to managers and ensure that managers demonstrate those values in their work.
- Executives participate on performance improvement teams and use quality tools and practices.
- Executives personally spend time with suppliers and customers.
- Executives personally mentor managers and ensure that promotion criteria reflect organizational values.
- Executives personally learn about the improvement practices of other organizations.
- Executives clearly articulate values (customer focus, customer satisfaction, role-model leadership, continuous improvement, involving the work force, and optimizing performance) throughout the organization.
- Executives base their business decisions on reliable data and facts pertaining to customers, operational processes, and employee performance and satisfaction.
- Executives ensure that organization values are used to provide direction to all employees in the organization to help achieve mission, vision, and quality goals.
- Executives hold regular meetings to review performance data and communicate problems, successes, and effective approaches to improve work.
- Executives use effective and innovative approaches to reach out to all employees to spread the organization's values and align its work to support organizational goals.
- Executives are open to surfacing problems and encourage employee risk taking.

B. Evaluation/Improvement

- Executives systematically and routinely check the effectiveness of their leadership activities: for example, seeking annual feedback from employees and peers (upward evaluation) and taking steps to improve.
- Executives conduct a monthly review of organizational and key supplier performance. This may require subordinates to conduct biweekly reviews, and workers and work teams to provide daily performance updates. Corrective actions are developed to improve performance that deviates from plan.

1.2 Leadership System and Organization (25 Points)

Describe how the company's customer focus and performance expectations are integrated into the company's leadership system, management, and organization.

Areas to Address:

a. How the company's values, expectations, and directions are integrated into its leadership system, management, and organization. Describe: (1) how the organization and its management of operations are designed to achieve companywide customer focus and commitment to high performance. Include roles and responsibilities of managers and supervisors; and (2) how values, expectations, and directions are effectively communicated and reinforced throughout the entire work force.

b. How overall company and work unit performance are reviewed. Include a description of: (1) the principal financial and nonfinancial measures used and how these measures relate to key stakeholders' primary needs and expectations; (2) how progress relative to plans is tracked; (3) how progress relative to competitors is tracked; (4) how asset productivity is determined; and (5) how review findings are used to set priorities for improvement actions.

Notes:

(1)   Reviews described in 1.2b might utilize information from business and customer-related results [Items 6.1, 6.2, 6.3, 6.4, and 7.4] and also might draw upon evaluations described in other Items and upon analysis [Item 2.3].

(2)   Reviews might include various economic measures as well as financial ones.

(3)   Assets [1.2b(4)] refers to human resources, materials, energy, capital, equipment, etc. Aggregate measures such as total factor productivity might also be used.

This item is scored using the **approach/deployment** scoring guidelines. It addresses how the company's leadership system creates an effective organization and management system—focused on overall performance.

Area 1.2a calls for information on how the company's organization, management, and work processes support its customer and performance objectives. This information should include the roles and responsibilities of managers and supervisors. Management needs to eliminate functional and management barriers that could lead to losing sight of customers and cause decision paths to be ineffective and slow. The area also calls for information on how the company's values, expectations, and directions are made real throughout the company via distributed leadership and effective communications. Communications need to include performance measures and objectives that help provide focus as well as alignment of company units.

Area 1.2b calls for information on how company and work unit performance is reviewed. Reviews are a primary means to communicate and reinforce what is really important, how performance is measured, and how well business objectives are being met. Reviews should include nonfinancial and financial information. Together, these types of information present a clear picture of status and trends relative to the company's key business drivers, the needs of all stakeholders, progress relative to competitors, and productivity of asset use. These are primary input data for setting improvement priorities.

Since a major purpose of reviews is to identify improvements and resource use priorities, the information for reviews needs to connect financial and operational data. Traditional cost accounting methods usually do not provide an adequate basis for targeting operational improvements that will lead to the most significant financial gains. Alternative accounting approaches such as activity-based costing might offer the best means to understand processes and activities in terms of true financial costs and benefits.

Such measures take into account all factors in production: human capacity, materials, capital, and assets. Approaches based upon economic indicators also provide useful information as they help determine whether or not performance improvements are contributing to wealth creation.

Important connections among operational customer-related, financial, and economic performance are addressed in Item 2.3.

1.2 Leadership System and Organization

How the organization's customer focus and performance expectations are integrated into the organization's leadership system and organization

Aligning the Leadership System and Organization

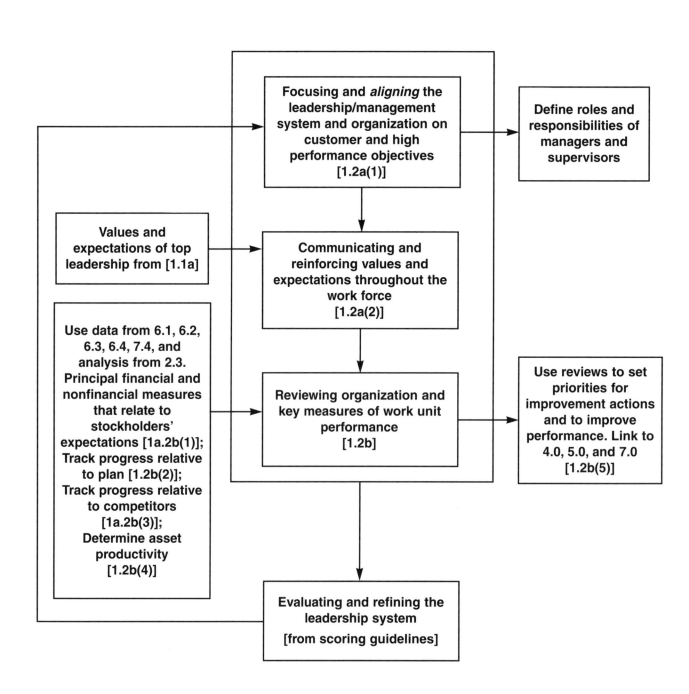

1.2 Leadership System and Organization Item Linkages

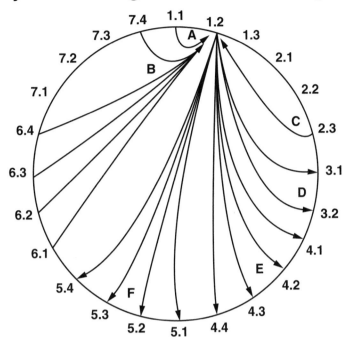

Item	Nature of Relationship
A	Senior executives [1.1] set, communicate, and cascade vision and quality values to managers throughout the organization [1.2a]; they set performance expectations [1.1b] and review conformance to plans [1.2c]. Senior executives [1.1a] provide a role model for managers to focus on customers and high performance objectives; they provide mentoring and rewards and recognition to managers [1.2a].
B	Business performance reviews [1.2b(5)] use information from business and customer results [6.1, 6.2, 6.3, 6.4, and 7.4].
C	Managers [1.2b] use data collected for decisions regarding allocation of resources and priorities to better serve customers [2.3a(1)], improve operating effectiveness [2.3a(2)] and competitive performance [2.3a(3)], and maximize financial returns [2.3b].
D	A broad base of managers participate in strategic planning [3.1] and in ensuring that the plans are deployed throughout the organization and used to align work at all levels [3.2].
E	Managers are responsible for optimizing the human resources of the organization including human resource planning [4.1]; improving performance and reward and recognition effectiveness [4.2]; training [4.3], and enhancing satisfaction and employee well-being [4.4].
F	Managers are responsible for creating an environment that supports high performance, including monitoring processes for design-build activities [5.1]; and for working with employees to improve operational performance [5.2], support services performance [5.3], and supplier performance [5.4].

1.2 Leadership System and Organization—Sample Effective Practices

A. Focusing on Customer and High Performance Objectives

- Roles and responsibilities of managers are clearly defined, understood by them, and used to judge their performance.
- Managers "walk-the-talk" in leading quality and systematic performance improvement.
- Job definitions with quality indices are clearly delineated for each level of the organization, objectively measured, and presented in a logical and organized structure.
- Many different communication strategies are used to reinforce quality values.
- Leader behavior clearly communicates what is expected.
- Systems and procedures are deployed that encourage cooperation and cross-functional approach to management, team activities, and problem solving.

B. Assessing Performance

- Leaders monitor employee acceptance and adoption of vision and values using annual surveys, employee focus groups, and E-mail questions.
- Reviews against measurable performance standards are held frequently.
- All departments hold reviews frequently (weekly, daily) to monitor progress toward measurable goals.
- Actions are taken to assist units that are not meeting goals and performing to plan.
- A systematic process is in place for evaluating the integration or alignment of quality values throughout the organization.
- Leaders at all levels determine how well they carried out their activities (what went right, wrong, and how it could be done better).
- There is evidence of adopting changes to improve.
- Priorities for improvement are driven by customer, performance, and financial data.

1.3 Public Responsibility and Corporate Citizenship (20 Points)

Describe how the company addresses its responsibilities to the public in its performance management practices. Describe also how the company leads and contributes as a corporate citizen in its key communities.

Areas to Address:

a. How the company integrates its public responsibilities into its performance improvement efforts. Describe: (1) the risks and regulatory and other legal requirements addressed in planning and in setting operational requirements, measures, and targets; (2) how the company looks ahead to anticipate public concerns and to assess possible impacts on society of its products, services, facilities, and operations; and (3) how the company promotes legal and ethical conduct in all that it does.

b. How the company leads and contributes as a corporate citizen in its key communities. Include a brief summary of the types of leadership and involvement the company emphasizes.

Notes:

(1) The public responsibility issues (1.3a) relate to the company's impacts and possible impacts on society associated with its products, services, facilities, and operations. They include environment, health, safety, and emergency preparedness as they relate to any aspect of risk or adverse effect, whether or not these are covered under law or regulation. Health and safety of employees are not addressed in Item 1.3. Employee health and safety are covered in Item 4.4.

(2) Major public responsibility or impact areas should also be addressed in planning (Item 3.1) and in the appropriate process management Items of Category 5.0. Key results, such as environmental improvements, should be reported in Item 6.2.

(3) If the company has received sanctions under law, regulation, or contract [1.3a(3)] during the past three years, briefly describe the incident(s) and its current status. If settlements have been negotiated in lieu of potential sanctions, give an explanation. If no sanctions have been received, so indicate.

(4) The corporate citizenship issues appropriate for inclusion in 1.3b relate to efforts by the company to strengthen community services, education, health care, environment, and practices of trade or business associations. Examples of corporate citizenship appropriate for inclusion in 1.3b are:

- *influencing and helping trade and business associations to create school-to-work programs;*
- *communicating employability requirements to schools;*
- *influencing national, state, and local policies which promote education improvement;*
- *partnering with and charitable giving to schools, e.g., sharing computers and computer expertise;*

Continued on next page

- developing trade and business consortia to improve environmental practices;
- promoting volunteerism among employees;
- partnering with other businesses and health care providers to improve health in the local community; and
- influencing trade and business associations to engage in cooperative activities to improve overall U.S. global competitiveness.

This item is scored using the **approach/deployment** scoring guidelines. It addresses how the company integrates its public responsibilities and corporate citizenship into its business planning and performance improvement practices.

Area 1.3a calls for information on three basic aspects of public responsibility: (1) making risk and legal requirements an integral part of performance improvement; (2) sensitivity in planning products, services, and operations to issues of societal concern, whether or not these issues are currently embodied in law; and (3) making legal and ethical conduct visible in the company's values and performance improvement processes. Fulfilling public responsibilities means not only meeting all local, state, and federal laws and regulatory requirements, but also treating these and related requirements as areas for improvement "beyond mere compliance." This means that the company should maintain constant awareness of potential public impacts related to its products, services, and operations.

Area 1.3b calls for information on how the company leads as a corporate citizen in its key communities. The issues in this area relate to the company as a member of different types of communities and being a positive influence upon other organizations. Opportunities for leadership and involvement include assistance by the company to strengthen community services, education, health care, the environment, and practices of trade and business associations. This includes community service by employees that is encouraged, supported, and recognized by the company. For example, companies and their employees could help to influence the adoption of higher standards in education or volunteer to assist as school partners.

1.3 Public Responsibility and Corporate Citizenship

Integrating Public Responsibility with Improvement Efforts

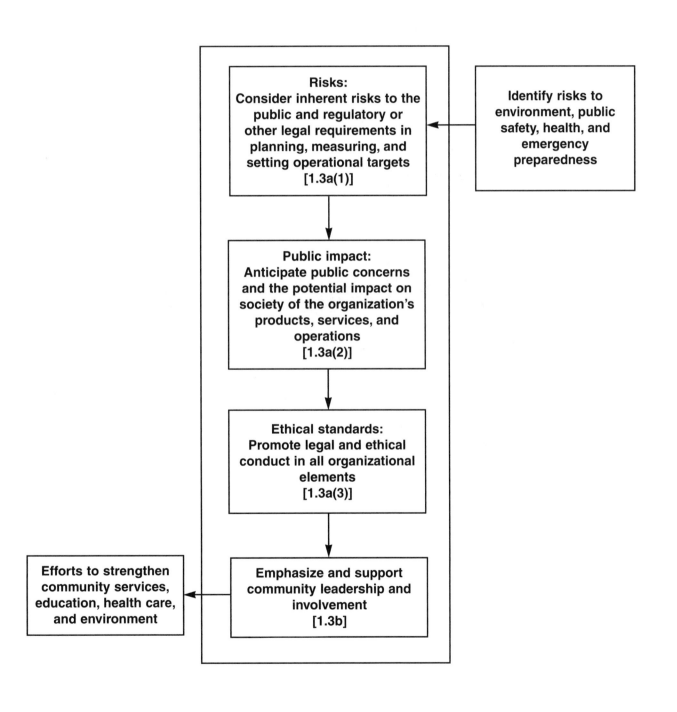

1.3 Public Responsibility and Corporate Citizenship Item Linkages

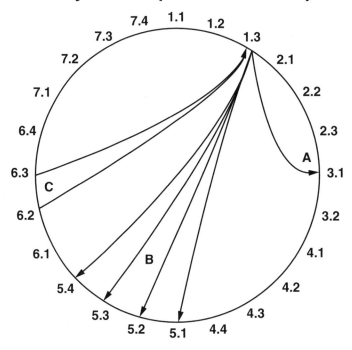

Item	Nature of Relationship
A	Public health and safety concerns, environmental protection, and waste management issues [1.3] may be important factors to consider in strategy development [3.1].
B	Managers at all levels have responsibility for ensuring that work practices of the organization [5.1, 5.2, and 5.3] and its suppliers [5.4] are consistent with the organization's standards of public responsibility described in [1.3].
C	Performance of the organization [6.2] and human resource results [6.3] are monitored in key areas of public responsibility, such as meeting statutory and regulatory requirements.

1.3 Public Responsibility and Corporate Citizenship— Sample Effective Practices

A. Integrates Quality Values and Public Responsibility

- The organization's principal business activities minimize public hazard or risk.
- Indicators for risk areas are identified.
- Continuous improvement strategies are used consistently and progress is reviewed regularly.
- The organization considers the impact its operations, products, and services might have on society and considers those impacts in planning.

B. Leaders as Corporate Citizens

- Employees at various levels in the organization are encouraged to be involved in professional organizations, committees, task forces, or teams dealing with quality.
- Organizational resources are allocated to support involvement in quality activities outside the organization.
- Employees participate in local, state, or national quality award programs and receive recognition from the organization.
- Employees participate in a variety of professional quality and business improvement associations.

2.0 Information and Analysis—75 Points

The Information and Analysis category examines the management and effectiveness of the use of data and information to support customer-driven performance excellence and marketplace success.

2.1 Management of Information and Data (20 Points)

Describe the company's selection and management of information and data used for strategic planning, management, and evaluation of overall performance.

Areas to Address:

a. How information and data needed to support operations and decision making and to drive improvement of overall company performance are selected and managed. Describe: (1) the main types of data and information and how each type supports key business operations and business strategy; (2) how the company's performance measurement system is designed to achieve alignment of operations with company priorities, such as key business drivers; and (3) how key requirements such as reliability, rapid access, and rapid update are derived from user needs and how the requirements are met.

b. How the company evaluates and improves the selection, analysis, and integration of information and data, aligning them with the company's key business drivers and operations. Describe how the evaluation considers: (1) scope of information and data; (2) use and analysis of information and data to support process management and performance improvement; and (3) feedback from users of information and data.

Notes:

(1) Reliability [2.1a(3)] includes software used in information systems.

(2) User needs [2.1a(3)] should consider knowledge accumulation such as knowledge about specific customers or customer segments. User needs should also take into account changing patterns of communications associated with changes in process management, job design, and business strategy.

(3) Feedback from users [2.1b(3)] might entail formal or informal surveys, focus groups, and teams. Factors in the evaluation might include completeness, timeliness, access, update, and reliability. The evaluation might also include assessment of the information technologies used.

This item is scored using the **approach/deployment** scoring guidelines. It addresses the company's selection and management of information and data to support overall business goals, with primary emphasis on supporting process management and performance improvement.

Area 2.1a calls for details on how information and data are selected and managed to drive improvement of overall company performance. The area has two parts. The first part addresses selection and emphasizes key business drivers—strategically important areas of performance that are crucial to company success. The second part addresses management of data and information, and emphasizes user needs—rapid access and update, and reliability.

Area 2.1b calls for information on how the company evaluates and improves its selection, analysis, and management of information and data. The area emphasizes alignment with business priorities, support of process management, and feedback from information and data users. The evaluation might take into account factors such as the extent and effectiveness of use, gaps in data, and organization of information and data.

Overall, Item 2.1 represents a key foundation for a performance-oriented company. This foundation should include nonfinancial information and data.

The main focus of Item 2.1 is on (the use of) information and data for effective performance management. Information, data, and information technology often have strategic significance as well. For example, information technology could be used to build and disseminate unique knowledge about customers and markets and to create the ability to operate more successfully in key markets. Also, information technology and the information and data made available through such technology could be of special advantage in business networks or alliances. Responses to Areas 2.1a and 2.1b should take into account such strategic use of information and data. Accordingly, *users* should then be interpreted as business partners as well as company units.

2.1 Management of Information and Data

Selection and management of information and data used for planning, decision making, and evaluation of overall performance

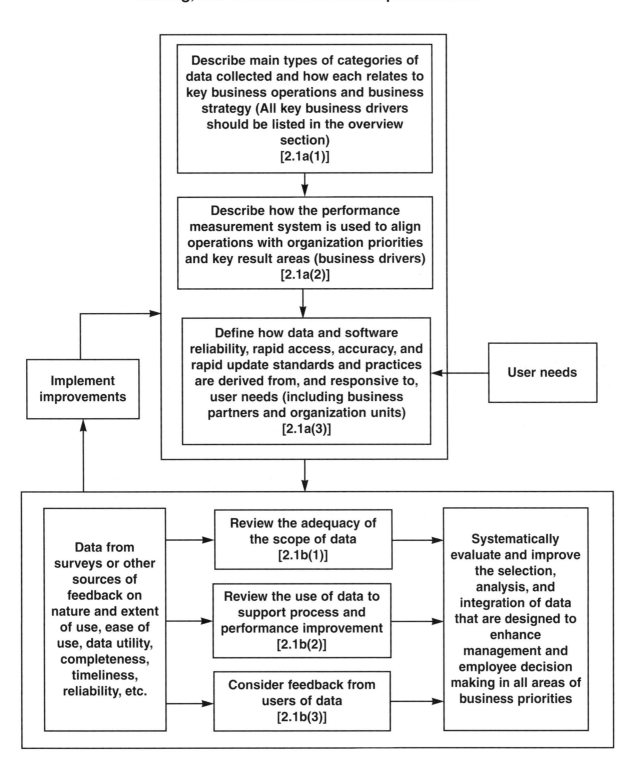

2.1 Management of Information and Data Item Linkages

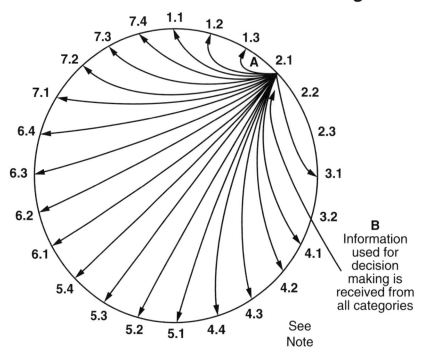

Item	Nature of Relationship
A	Information collected [2.1] is used for planning [3.1], day-to-day management [1.1 and 1.2], setting community responsibility standards [1.3], monitoring of quality and operational performance [6.1, 6.2, 6.3, 6.4], improving work processes [5.1, 5.2, 5.3, 5.4] and human resource performance [4.1, 4.2, 4.3, 4.4], determining customer requirements [7.1], building customer relations [7.2], and determining [7.3] and reporting customer satisfaction [7.4].
B	Information used for management decision making and continuous improvement [2.1] is collected from all categories.

NOTE: Because the information collected and used for decision making links with all other Items, the linkage arrows will not all be repeated on the other item maps. The more relevant connections will be identified.

2.1 Management of Information and Data—Sample Effective Practices

A. Data Types and Scope

- Data collected at the individual worker level are consistent across the organization to permit consolidation and organization-wide performance monitoring.
- Quality and operational data are collected and used for management decisions.
- Internal and external data are used to describe customer satisfaction and product and service performance.
- The costs of quality and other financial concerns are measured for internal operations and processes.
- Data are maintained on employee-related issues of satisfaction, morale, safety, education and training, use of teams, and recognition and reward.
- Supplier quality data are maintained.
- The data collection and analysis system is periodically evaluated.
- Refinements have been made to reduce cycle time for data collection and increase data access and use.

B. Improving Data Selection, Analysis, and Integration

- Various techniques are used to ensure data reliability and objectivity.
- Employees, customers, and suppliers are involved in validating data.
- A systematic process exists for data review and improvement, standardization, and easy employee access to data. Training on the use of data systems is provided as needed.
- Data used for management decisions focus on key business drivers and are integrated in work processes for the planning, design, and delivery of products and services.

2.2 Competitive Comparisons and Benchmarking (15 Points)

Describe the company's processes and uses of comparative information and data to support improvement of overall performance and competitive position.

Areas to Address:

a. How competitive comparisons and benchmarking information and data are selected and used to help drive improvement of overall company performance. Describe: (1) how needs and priorities are determined; (2) criteria for seeking appropriate information and data—from within and outside the company's industry and markets; (3) how the information and data are used to improve understanding of processes and process performance; and (4) how the information and data are used to set stretch targets and/or to encourage breakthrough approaches aligned with the company's competitive strategy.

b. How the company evaluates and improves its process for selecting and using competitive comparisons and benchmarking information and data to improve planning, overall company performance, and competitive position.

Notes:

(1) Benchmarking information and data refer to processes and results that represent best practices and performance, inside or outside of the company's industry. Competitive comparisons refer to performance levels relative to direct competitors in the company's markets.

(2) Needs and priorities [2.2a(1)] should show clear linkage to the company's key business drivers.

(3) Use of benchmarking information and data within the company [2.2a(3)] might include the expectation that company units maintain awareness of related best-in-class performance to help drive improvement. This could entail education and training efforts to build capabilities.

(4) Sources of competitive comparisons and benchmarking information might include: (a) information obtained from other organizations such as customers or suppliers through sharing; (b) information obtained from the open literature; (c) testing and evaluation by the company itself; and (d) testing and evaluation by independent organizations.

(5) The evaluation (2.2b) may address a variety of factors such as the effectiveness of use of the information, adequacy of information, training in acquisition and use of information, improvement potential in company operations, and estimated rates of improvement by other organizations.

This item is scored using the **approach/deployment** scoring guidelines. It addresses external drivers of improvement—data and information related to competitive position and to best practices. Such data may have both operational and strategic value.

The major premises underlying this item are: (1) companies need to know where they stand relative to competitors and to best-practice performance for similar activities; (2) comparative and benchmarking information provides impetus for significant (breakthrough) improvement and alerts companies to competitive threats and new practices; and (3) companies need to understand their own processes and the processes of others before they compare performance levels.

Benchmarking information may also support business analysis and decisions relating to core competencies, alliances, and outsourcing.

Area 2.2a calls for information on how competitive comparisons and benchmarking data are selected and used to help drive improvement of overall company performance. The area focuses on priorities and criteria for selecting benchmarking information and data. The area also examines the use of data to set stretch goals and to develop an understanding of processes and process performance techniques.

Area 2.2b calls for information on how the company evaluates and improves its processes for selecting and using competitive and benchmark information to drive performance improvement.

2.2 Competitive Comparisons and Benchmarking

**Processes and uses of comparative information and data
to support improvement of overall performance**

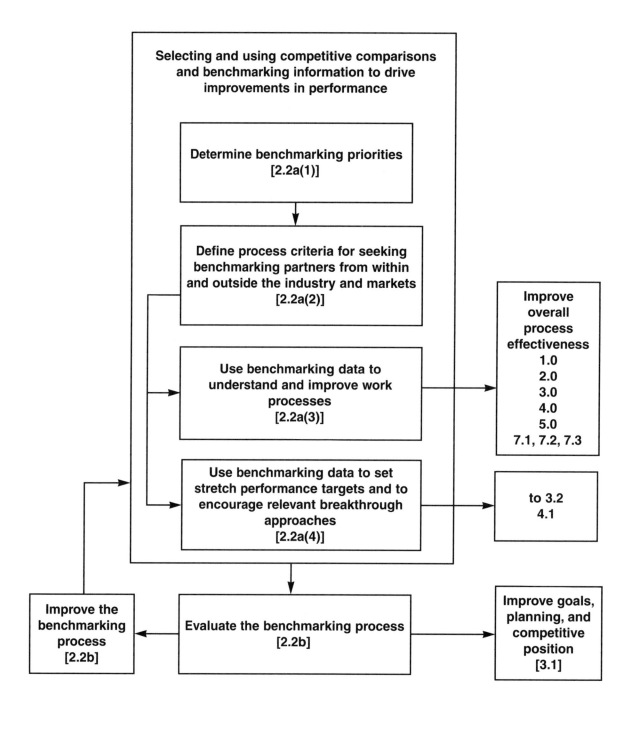

2.2 Competitive Comparisons and Benchmarking Item Linkages

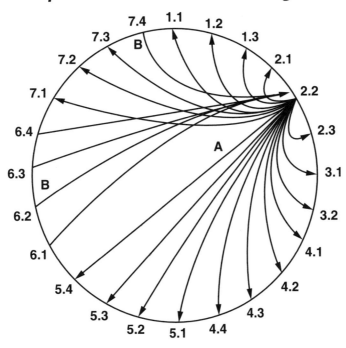

Item	Nature of Relationship
A	Benchmark and comparison data [2.2] can be used to improve data collection, benchmarking, data analysis [2.1, 2.2, 2.3], and leadership effectiveness [Category 1.0]; to encourage breakthrough improvements in customer-related areas [7.1, 7.2, 7.3]; in design and introduction of products and services [5.1], product and service production and delivery [5.2], support services [5.3], and supplier performance [5.4]; for planning [3.1] and to set stretch objectives and goals [3.2]; and to improve employee morale [4.4], employee performance and reward and recognition [4.2], human resources planning [4.1], and training [4.3].
B	The need for information to help set priorities for selecting benchmarking and comparison organizations [2.2] is driven by work processes that need improvement [Category 5.0] as determined by Category 6.0 results and Item 7.4 results. Benchmarking targets may also be driven by the need to improve leadership, planning, human resource management activities, and customer focus and satisfaction processes [7.1, 7.2, and 7.3].

NOTE: Because benchmarking information links with most items, the linkage arrows will not be repeated on all other item maps; however, the most relevant connections will be identified.

2.2 Competitive Comparisons and Benchmarking— Sample Effective Practices

A. Selection Criteria and Rationale

- A systematic process is in place for identifying benchmark targets.
- Research has been conducted to identify best-in-class organizations, which may be competitors or noncompetitors.
- Key processes or functions are the subject of benchmarking. Activities such as those that support the organization's goals and objectives are the subject of benchmarking.
- Benchmarking covers key products, services, customer satisfiers, suppliers, employees, and support operations.
- The organization reaches beyond its own business to conduct benchmarking studies.
- Benchmark or comparison data are used to improve the understanding of work processes and to discover the best levels of performance that have been achieved. Based on this knowledge, the organization sets goals or targets to stretch performance.

B. Evaluation and Improvement

- A systematic approach is used to evaluate and improve processes for selecting, gathering, and using benchmark data.
- Benchmarking processes are fully documented.
- Systematic actions have been taken to improve the quality and use of benchmark data, including the use of comparison data in a goal setting (Item 3.2).

2.3 Analysis and Use of Company-Level Data (40 Points)

Describe how data related to quality, customers, and operational performance, together with relevant financial data, are analyzed to support company-level review, action, and planning.

Areas to Address:

a. How information and data from all parts of the company are integrated and analyzed to support reviews, business decisions, and planning. Describe how analysis is used to gain understanding of: (1) customers and markets; (2) operational performance and company capabilities; and (3) competitive performance.

b. How the company relates customer and market data, improvement in product/service quality, and improvements in operational performance to changes in financial and/or market indicators of performance. Describe how this information is used to set priorities for improvement actions.

Notes:

(1) Item 2.3 focuses primarily on analysis for company-level purposes, such as reviews (Item 1.2b) and strategic planning (Item 3.1). Data for such analysis come from all parts of the company and include results reported in Items 6.1, 6.2, 6.3, 6.4, and 7.4. Other Items call for analyses of specific sets of data for special purposes. For example, the Items of Category 4.0 require analysis to determine effectiveness of training and other human resource practices. Such special-purpose analyses should be part of the overall information base available for use in Item 2.3.

(2) Analysis includes trends, projections, cause-effect correlations, and the search for deeper understanding needed to set priorities to use resources more effectively to serve overall business objectives. Accordingly, analysis draws upon all kinds of data: operational, customer-related, financial, and economic.

(3) Examples of analysis appropriate for inclusion in 2.3a(1) are:
   - *how the company's product and service quality improvement correlates with key customer indicators such as customer satisfaction, customer retention, and market share;*
   - *cost/revenue implications of customer-related problems and problem resolution effectiveness; and*
   - *interpretation of market share changes in terms of customer gains and losses and changes in customer satisfaction.*

Continued on next page

(4) Examples of analysis appropriate for inclusion in 2.3a(2) are:
- *trends in improvement in key operational indicators such as productivity, cycle time, waste reduction, new product introduction, and defect levels;*
- *financial benefits from improved employee safety, absenteeism, and turnover;*
- *benefits and costs associated with education and training;*
- *how the company's ability to identify and meet employee requirements correlates with employee retention, motivation, and productivity;*
- *cost/revenue implications of employee-related problems and problem resolution effectiveness; and*
- *trends in individual measures of productivity such as manpower productivity.*

(5) Examples of analysis appropriate for inclusion in 2.3a(3) are:
- *working capital productivity relative to competitors;*
- *individual or aggregate measures of productivity relative to competitors;*
- *performance trends relative to competitors on key quality attributes; and*
- *cost trends relative to competitors.*

(6) Examples of analysis appropriate for inclusion in 2.3b are:
- *relationships between product/service quality and operational performance indicators and overall company financial performance trends as reflected in indicators such as operating costs, revenues, asset utilization, and value added per employee;*
- *allocation of resources among alternative improvement projects based on cost/revenue implications and improvement potential;*
- *net earnings derived from quality/operational/human resource performance improvements;*
- *comparisons among business units showing how quality and operational performance improvement affect financial performance;*
- *contributions of improvement activities to cash flow and/or shareholder value;*
- *profit impacts of customer retention;*
- *market share versus profits;*
- *trends in aggregate measures such as total factor productivity; and*
- *trends in economic and/or market indicators of value.*

This item is scored using the **approach/deployment** scoring guidelines. It addresses company-level analysis—the principal basis for guiding a company's process management toward business results. Despite the importance of individual facts and data, by themselves they do not usually provide a sound basis for actions or priorities. Action depends upon understanding cause and effect connections among processes and between processes and business results. Process actions may have many resource implications; achieving desired results may have many cost and revenue implications as well. Given that resources for improvement are limited, and cause and effect connections are often unclear, there is a critical need to provide a sound analytical basis for decisions. In the criteria, this role is served by analyses of many types. Item 2.3 plays the key linkage role in an integrated data and analysis system that is built around financial and nonfinancial data.

Area 2.3a calls for information on how data and information from all parts of the company are aggregated and analyzed to support reviews, business decisions, and planning. The focus is on three key areas of performance: customers and markets, operational performance, and competitive performance. The analyses in this area depend upon nonfinancial and financial data, which are connected to provide a basis for decision making and action.

Area 2.3b calls for analysis linking customer and market data, improvements in product and service quality, and improvements in operational performance to improvement in financial or market indicators. The purpose of this linkage is to guide the selection of effective improvement efforts, to achieve revenue growth, and to reduce operating costs.

2.3 Analysis and Use of Company-Level Data

How data related to quality, customers, and operational performance, together with relevant financial data, are analyzed to support company-level review, action, and planning

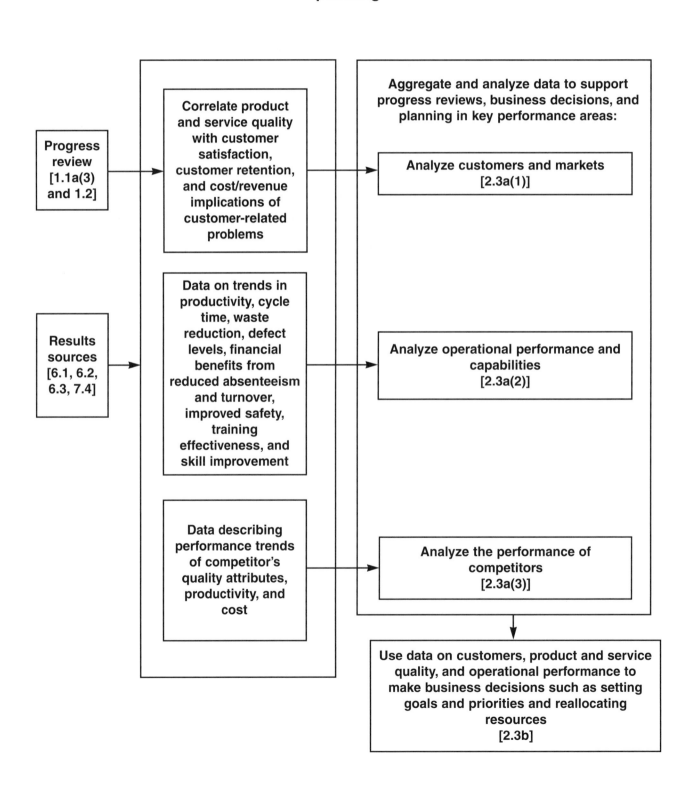

2.3 Analysis and Use of Company-Level Data Item Linkages

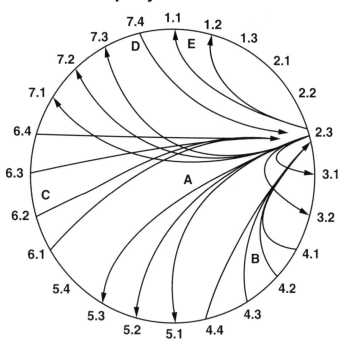

Item	Nature of Relationship
A	Data are aggregated and analyzed in [2.3] to set priorities such as: [2.3a(1)] developing solutions to customer problems [7.2], determining the best ways to assess customer satisfaction trends [7.3] and requirements [7.1]; [2.3a(2)] targeting processes to improve [5.1, 5.2, 5.3] that will reduce cycle time, waste, and defect levels, and improve safety, absenteeism, employee retention, and financial performance; and [2.3a(3)] understanding competitive performance; and providing input to the planning process [3.1] and for goal setting [3.2].
B	Information regarding human resources development plans [4.1] is used to support reviews, business decisions, and planning. Information regarding human resources capabilities, including involvement and recognition [4.2], training [4.3], and well-being and satisfaction [4.4] is used to set priorities for improvement actions [2.3b].
C	Information regarding operating performance [Category 6.0] is used to gain an understanding of operational performance and capabilities [2.3a(2)], and to set priorities and allocate resources to improve operating efficiency [2.3a(2)].
D	Information regarding actual customer satisfaction results [7.4] is used to gain an understanding of customers, markets, and competitive performance [2.3a(1)], and set priorities and allocate resources to improve performance [2.3c].
E	Leaders at all levels [1.1 and 1.2] have responsibility for analyzing data [2.3] for purposes of resource allocation and priority setting.

2.3 Analysis and Use of Company-Level Data— Sample Effective Practices

A. Data Analysis

- Systematic processes are in place for analyzing customer-related data and results (including complaint data), and setting priorities for action.
- Facts, rather than intuition, are used to support decision making at all levels.
- The analysis process itself is analyzed to make the results more timely and useful for top-level decision making for quality improvement.
- Analysis processes and tools, and the value of analyses to decision making, are systematically evaluated and improved.

B. Data Uses

- Customer and operational performance data, including financial performance data, are used to support performance reviews, planning, and resource allocation.
- Data are used to help leaders improve operations-related decision making (such as determining improvement priorities); evaluating the cost impact of improvement initiatives and trends in key operational indicators (such as cycle time, waste and rework, and product/service quality); and using benchmark data to set improvement priorities and targets.
- Data regarding improvements in performance and financial performance are used in planning, goal setting, and establishing priorities.
- The impacts of improvement activities on customer satisfaction, operational effectiveness, and financial indicators (for example, operating costs, production value per employee, cost per employee) are used to set improvement priorities.

3.0 Strategic Planning—55 Points

The Strategic Planning category examines how the company sets strategic direction and how it determines key plan requirements. Also examined is how the plan requirements are translated into an effective performance management system.

3.1 Strategy Development (35 Points)

Describe the company's strategic planning process for overall performance and competitive leadership for the short term and the longer term. Describe also how this process leads to the development of a basis (key business drivers) for deploying plan requirements throughout the company.

Areas to Address:

a. How the company develops strategies and business plans to strengthen its customer-related, operational, and financial performance and its competitive position. Describe how strategy development considers: (1) customer requirements and expectations and their expected changes; (2) the competitive environment; (3) risks: financial, market, technological, and societal; (4) company capabilities—human resource, technology, research and development, and business processes—to seek new market leadership opportunities and/or to prepare for key new requirements; and (5) supplier and/or partner capabilities.

b. How strategies and plans are translated into actionable key business drivers.

c. How the company evaluates and improves its strategic planning and plan deployment processes.

Continued on next page

Notes:

(1)   Item 3.1 addresses overall company strategy and business plans, not specific product and service designs.

(2)   Strategy and planning refer to a future-oriented basis for major business decisions, resource allocations, and companywide management. Strategy and planning, then, address both revenue growth thrusts as well as thrusts related to improving company performance. The sub-parts of 3.1a are intended to serve as an outline of key factors involved in developing a view of the future as a context for strategic planning.

(3)   Customer requirements and their expected changes [3.1a(1)] might include pricing factors. That is, competitive success may depend upon achieving cost levels dictated by anticipated market prices rather than setting prices to cover costs.

(4)   The purposes of projecting the competitive environment [3.1a(2)] are to detect and reduce competitive threats, to shorten reaction time, and to identify opportunities. If the company uses modeling, scenario, or other techniques to project the competitive environment, such techniques should be briefly outlined in 3.1a(2).

(5)   Key business drivers are the areas of performance most critical to the company's success. The purpose of the key business drivers is to ensure that strategic planning leads to a pragmatic basis for deployment, communications, and assessment of progress. Actual key business drivers should not be described in 3.1b. Such information is requested in Item 3.2, which focuses on deployment.

(6)   How the company evaluates and improves its strategic planning and plan deployment process might take into account the results of reviews (1.2b), input from work units, and projection information (3.2b). The evaluation might also take into account how well strategies and requirements are communicated and understood, and how well key measures throughout the company are aligned.

This item is scored using the **approach/deployment** scoring guidelines. It addresses how the company develops its vision of the future, sets strategic direction, and translates this direction into actionable key business drivers, including customer satisfaction and market leadership requirements. The focus of the item is on competitive leadership. Such leadership depends upon revenue growth as well as on operational effectiveness.

Area 3.1a calls for information on the key influences, challenges, and requirements that might affect the company's future opportunities and directions—*taking as long a view as possible*. The main purpose of the area is to develop a thorough and realistic context for the development of a customer- and market-focused strategy to guide ongoing decision making, resource allocation, and companywide management.

Area 3.1b calls for information on how strategy and plans are translated into actionable key business drivers, which serve as the basis for operationalizing and deploying plan requirements, addressed in Item 3.2. This translation might include a determination of activities the company should perform itself and those for which it might use or seek partners.

Area 3.1c calls for information on how the company evaluates and improves its strategic planning and plan deployment processes. This might involve input from work units regarding key deployment factors, such as effective translation and communication of strategy and plans, adequacy of resources, and key new needs.

Item 3.1 plays a central directional role in the criteria. These activities focus company leadership on developing a competitive strategy and on operationalizing this strategy. This requires the creation of a view of the future that takes into account not only the markets or segments to compete in but also how to compete. "How to compete" presents many options and requires a solid understanding of the company's and competitors' strengths and weaknesses. Operationalizing the strategy in the form of key business drivers is intended to highlight the importance of clear and measurable performance objectives. These objectives serve to guide the design and management of key processes. The objectives may also serve to align communications, compensation, and recognition systems with performance objectives.

3.1 Strategy Development

Strategic planning process for overall performance and competitive leadership for the short term and the longer term

SWOT Analysis—Strategic Planning Process

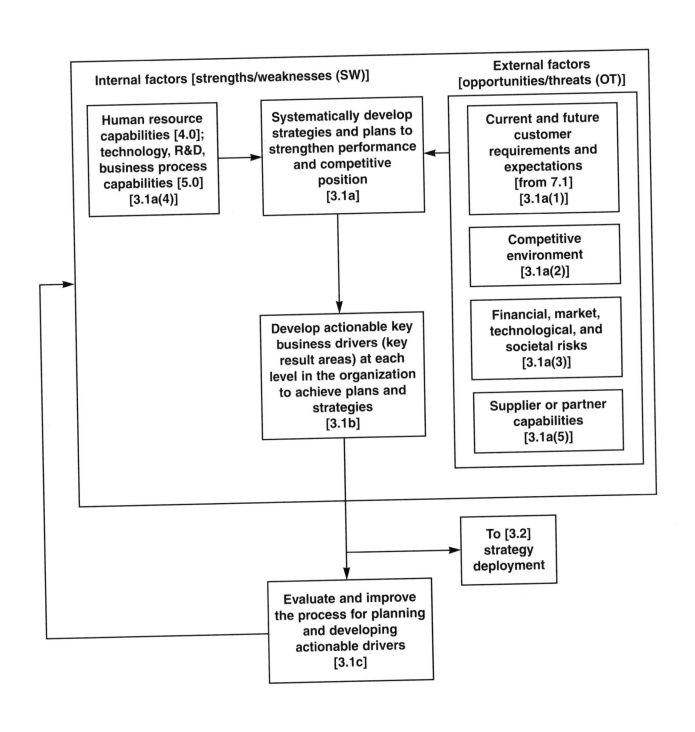

3.1 Strategy Development Item Linkages

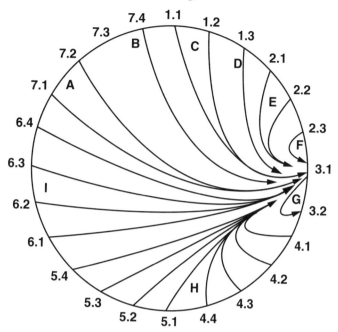

Item	Nature of Relationship
A	The business planning process includes information on current and *future* customer requirements and the projected competitive environment [7.1] as well as intelligence obtained from customer contact people [7.2].
B	Customer satisfaction and competitor results [7.4] data are critical to planning [3.1] broken out by competitor/market.
C	The planning process [3.1] includes senior executive [1.1] participation and guidance as well as participation by leaders at all levels [1.2].
D	Public health, environmental, waste management, and related concerns [1.3] are considered, as appropriate, in the strategy development process [3.1].
E	Key organizational [2.1] and competitive comparison data [2.2] are used for planning [3.1].
F	Organizational priorities [2.3] including work process improvement strategies, realigning work processes, improving operational performance, and reducing waste are used in the planning process [3.1].
G	The planning process [3.1] produces a plan [3.2] and sets of actionable items.
H	Information on human resource capabilities [4.0] and work process capabilities [5.0] are considered in the strategic planning process.
I	Organization performance and supplier quality results [6.0] are used in the planning process [3.1] to set priorities and goals [3.2].
Note:	The many inputs to strategy development will not all be repeated on other linkage diagrams to avoid clutter.

3.1 Strategy Development—Sample Effective Practices

A. Goal-Setting Process for Performance Improvement

- Business goals, strategies, and issues are addressed in short-term (1–3 year) and long-term (3+ year) plans. Goals consider future requirements for achieving organizational leadership after considering the quality levels other organizations are likely to achieve.
- The planning and goal setting process encourages input (but not necessarily decision making) from a variety of people at all levels throughout the organization.
- Data on customer requirements, key markets, benchmarks, supplier capabilities, and organizational capabilities are used to develop business plans.
- Plans are in place to optimize operational performance and improve customer focus using tools such as reengineering, streamlining work processes, and reducing cycle time.

B. From Plans to Actions

- Business plans, short- and long-term goals, and performance measures are understood and used to drive actions throughout the organization.
- Each individual in the organization, at all levels, understands how his or her work contributes to achieving organizational goals and plans.
- Plans are followed to ensure that resources are deployed and redeployed as needed to support goals.
- Capital projects are funded according to business improvement plans.

C. Evaluation and Improvement

- Plans are evaluated each cycle for accuracy and completeness.
- Opportunities for improvement in the planning process are identified systematically and carried out with each planning cycle.
- Refinements in the process of planning, plan deployment, and receiving input from work units have been made. Improvements in plan cycle time, plan resources, and planning accuracy are documented.

This item addresses how the company's key business drivers are used to align the work of the organization to achieve goals. Also addressed is a projection of key measures of the company's performance and the performance of competitors. The main intent of the item is to focus all work units on effective operationalizing of the key business drivers, including the use of measures that permit the tracking of performance.

3.2 Strategy Deployment (20 Points)

Summarize the company's key business drivers and how they are deployed. Show how the company's performance projects into the future relative to competitors and key benchmarks.

Areas to Address:

a. Summary of the specific key business drivers derived from the company's strategic direction and how these drivers are translated into actions. Describe: (1) key performance requirements and associated operational performance measures and/or indicators and how they are deployed; (2) how the company aligns work unit and supplier and/or partner plans and targets; (3) how productivity and cycle time improvement and reduction in waste are included in plans and targets; and (4) the principal resources committed to the accomplishment of plans. Note any important distinctions between short-term plans and longer-term plans.

b. Two-to-five year projection of key measures and/or indicators of the company's customer-related and operational performance. Describe how product and/or service quality and operational performance might be expected to compare with key competitors and key benchmarks over this time period. Briefly explain the comparisons, including any estimates or assumptions made regarding the projected product and/or service quality and operational performance of competitors or changes in key benchmarks.

Notes:

(1) The focus in Item 3.2 is on the translation of the company's strategic plans, resulting from the process described in Item 3.1, to requirements for work units, suppliers, and partners. The main intent of Item 3.2 is effective alignment of short- and long-term operations with strategic directions. Although the deployment of these plans will affect products and services, design of products and services is not the focus of Item 3.2. Such design is addressed in Item 5.1.

(2) Productivity and cycle time improvement and waste reduction [3.2a(3)] might address factors such as inventories, operational complexity, work-in-process, inspection, downtime, changeover time, set-up time, and other examples of utilization of resources—materials, equipment, energy, capital, and labor.

(3) Area 3.2b addresses projected progress in improving performance and in gaining advantage relative to competitors. This projection may draw upon analysis [Item 2.3] and data reported in results Items [Category 6.0 and Item 7.4]. Such projections are intended to support reviews [1.2b], evaluation of planning [3.1c], and other Items. Another purpose is to take account of the fact that competitors and benchmarks may also be improving over the time period of the projection.

(4) Projections of customer-related and operational performance [3.2b] might be expressed in terms of costs, revenues, measures of productivity, and economic indicators. Projections might also include innovation rates or other factors important to the company's competitive position.

This item is scored using the **approach/deployment** scoring guidelines.

Area 3.2a calls for information on the company's key business drivers and how these drivers are translated into an action plan. This includes spelling out key performance requirements; alignment of work unit, supplier, and partner plans; how productivity, cycle time, and waste reduction are addressed; and the principal resources committed to the accomplishment of plans. Alignment of the daily work of all units provides the discipline and consistent focus for ongoing improvement activities.

Area 3.2b calls for a projection of key measures and indicators of the company's quality and operational performance. It also calls for comparing projected company performance with that of competitors and key benchmarks. This projection/comparison is intended to encourage companies to improve their understanding of dynamic, competitive quality and operational performance factors, and to take into account their competitors' rates of improvement as a diagnostic management tool.

3.2 Strategy Deployment

**How the work of the organization is aligned to achieve
the goals of the strategic plan**

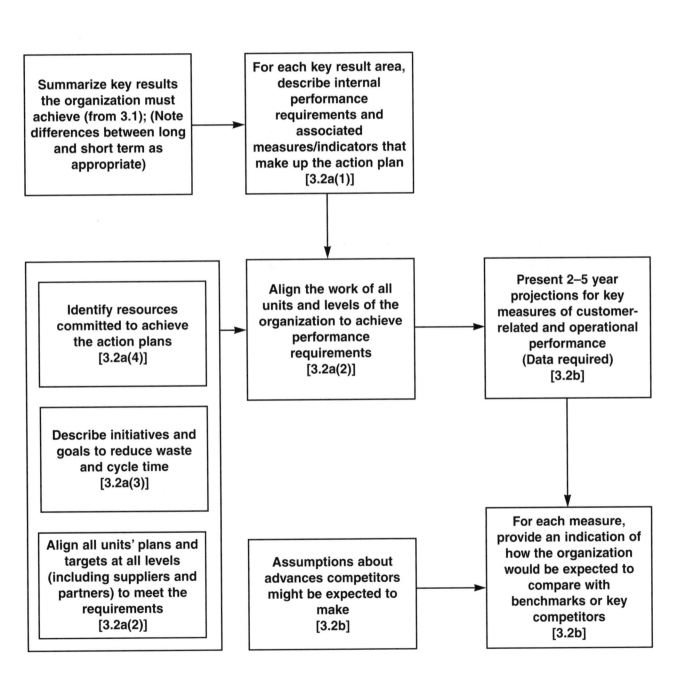

3.2 Strategy Deployment Item Linkages

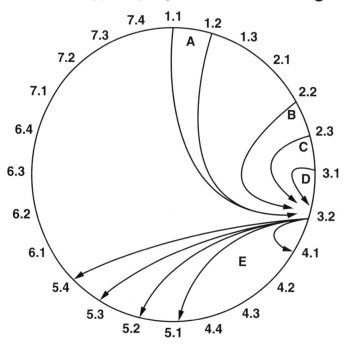

Item	Nature of Relationship
A	The organization's goals and objectives [3.2] are approved by senior executives [1.1] and by leaders throughout the organization [1.2].
B	Benchmarking comparison data [2.2] are used to set organizational measures and objectives [3.2].
C	Data analyzed [2.3] are used to help prioritize goals and objectives [3.2].
D	The strategic and operational plan [3.2] results from the planning process [3.1].
E	Measures, objectives, and plans, deployed to the work force, are used to drive and align actions to achieve improved performance [5.0] and develop human resource plans [4.1].

Note: The plan may also affect community responsibility actions [1.3], data and measures that need to be collected to monitor alignment [2.1], customer relations management [7.2], and customer satisfaction determination [7.3].

3.2 Strategy Deployment—Sample Effective Practices

A. Business Drivers

- Strategies to retain or establish leadership positions exist for major products and services for key customers or markets.
- Strategies to achieve key organizational results (operational performance requirements) are defined.
- Planned quality levels are defined for key features of products and services.
- Planned actions are challenging, realistic, achievable, and understood by employees throughout the organization. Each employee understands his or her role in achieving strategic and operational goals and objectives.
- Resources are available and committed to achieve the plans (no unfunded mandates).
- Long-term plans are realistic and used to guide quality and operational performance improvements.
- Incremental (short-term) strategies to achieve long-term plans are defined.

B. Projections and Comparisons

- Projections of two- to five-year changes in performance levels are developed and used to track progress.
- Data from competitors and key benchmarks form a basis for comparison. The organization has strategies and goals in place to exceed the planned levels of quality and performance for these competitors and benchmarks.

4.0 Human Resource Development and Management—140 Points

The Human Resource Development and Management category examines how the work force is enabled to develop and utilize its full potential, aligned with the company's performance objectives. Also examined are the company's efforts to build and maintain an environment for quality excellence conducive to performance excellence, full participation, and personal and organizational growth.

4.1 Human Resource Planning and Evaluation (20 Points)

Describe how the company's human resource planning and evaluation are aligned with its strategic and business plans and address the development and well-being of the entire work force.

Areas to Address:

a. How the company translates overall requirements from strategic and business planning [Category 3.0] to specific human resource plans. Summarize key human resource plans in the following areas: (1) changes in work design to improve flexibility, innovation, and rapid response; (2) employee development, education, and training; (3) changes in compensation, recognition, and benefits; and (4) recruitment, including critical skill categories and expected or planned changes in demographics of the work force. Distinguish between the short term and the longer term, as appropriate.

b. How the company evaluates and improves its human resource planning and practices and the alignment of the plans and practices with the company's strategic and business direction. Include how employee-related data and company performance data (Item 6.2) are analyzed and used: (1) to assess the development and well-being of all categories and types of employees; (2) to assess the linkage of the human resource practices to key business results; and (3) to ensure that reliable and complete human resource information is available for company planning and recruitment.

Continued on next page

Notes:

(1) Human resource planning addresses all aspects of designing and managing human systems to meet the needs of both the company and the employees. This Item calls for information on human resource plans. Examples of human resource plan [4.1a] elements that might be part(s) of a comprehensive plan are:

- *redesign of work organizations and/or jobs to increase employee responsibility and decision making;*
- *initiatives to promote labor-management cooperation, such as partnerships with unions;*
- *creation or modification of compensation and recognition systems based on building shareholder value and/or customer satisfaction;*
- *creation or redesign of employee surveys to better assess the factors in the work climate that contribute to or inhibit high performance;*
- *prioritization of employee problems based upon potential impact on productivity;*
- *development of hiring criteria and/or standards;*
- *creation of opportunities for employees to learn and use skills that go beyond current job assignments through redesign of processes or organizations;*
- *education and training initiatives, including those that involve developmental assignments;*
- *formation of partnerships with educational institutions to develop employees or to help ensure the future supply of well-prepared employees;*
- *establishment of partnerships with other companies and/or networks to share training and/or spread job opportunities;*
- *introduction of distance learning or other technology-based learning approaches; and*
- *integration of customer and employee surveys.*

(2) "Employee-related data" (4.1b) refers to data contained in personnel records as well as data described in Items 4.2, 4.3, 4.4, and 6.3. This might include employee satisfaction data and data on turnover, absenteeism, safety, grievances, involvement, recognition, training, and information from exit interviews.

(3) "Categories of employees" [4.1b(1)] refers to the company's classification system used in its human resource practices and/or work assignments. It also includes factors such as union or bargaining unit membership. "Types of employees" takes into account other factors, such as work force diversity or demographic makeup. This includes gender, age, minorities, and the disabled.

(4) Human resource information for company planning and recruitment [4.1b(3)] might include an overall profile of strengths and weaknesses that could affect the company's capabilities to fulfill plan requirements.

This item is scored using the **approach/deployment** scoring guidelines. It serves as the point of direct linkage between human resource planning and the company's strategic goals. Human resource planning should address the development of the entire work force and the needs of a high performance workplace. The item addresses how the company aligns its human resource planning and practices with its strategic plans so that high performance workplace practices become part of a coordinated organizational strategy. This item calls for information on the organization's *future* human resource plans that will position the work force to achieve the organization's future strategic goals.

Area 4.1a calls for information on key human resource plans derived from company strategic and business planning. The area calls for the primary thrusts, broadly defined, of the company's human resource plans—the ones needed to support its overall strategic direction. This is intended to provide a multiyear context and guide for human resource planning, management, and evaluation.

Area 4.1b calls for information on how the company evaluates and improves its overall human resource planning and management. This area is the brain center for human resource processes and results, as it relies upon employee-related and company performance data and information, and ties the overall evaluation to company strategy and business results. However, the evaluation also must go beyond broad strategy to the essential details of human resource effectiveness. The evaluation needs to provide the company's senior executives with information on strengths and weaknesses in human resource practices and development that might bear upon the company's abilities to achieve its short-term and longer-term business objectives. For example, the evaluation should take into account the development and progression of all categories and types of employees, including new employees. This information should be considered as a part of strategic planning.

The evaluation should also monitor the extent of deployment of education and training throughout the company and how well education and training support company performance improvement [Item 4.3]. The overall evaluation needs to rely heavily upon the well-being and satisfaction factors addressed in Item 4.4.

4.1 Human Resource Planning and Evaluation

How the company's human resource planning and evaluation are aligned with its strategic and business plans and address the development and well-being of the entire work force

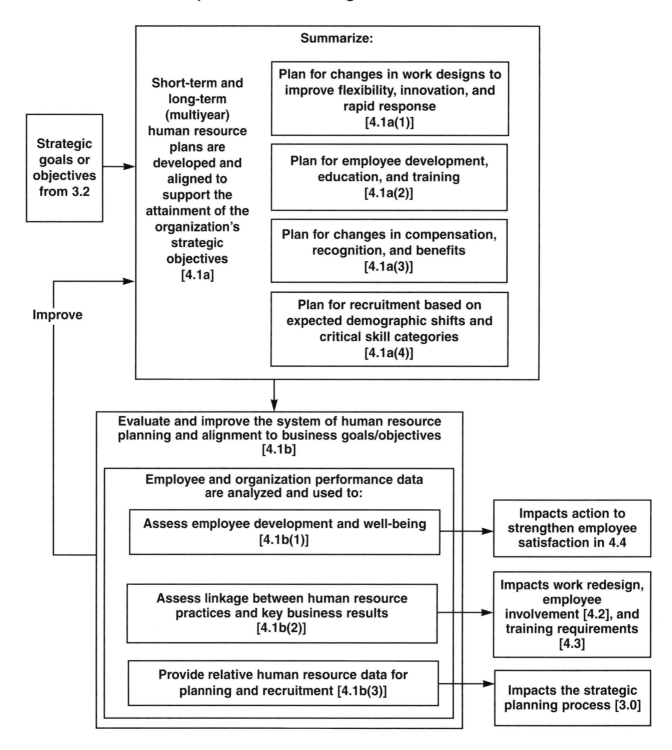

4.1 Human Resource Planning and Evaluation Item Linkages

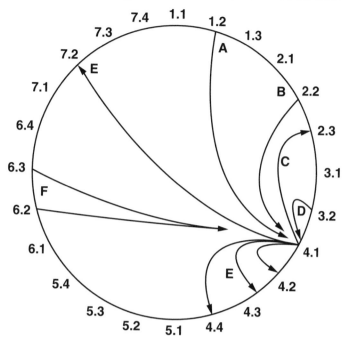

Item	Nature of Relationship
A	Managers throughout the organization [1.1 and 1.2] are responsible for ensuring that human resource plans and goals enhance work force performance and eliminating barriers to optimum work.
B	Human resource development and performance goals are influenced by data collected on benchmark results [2.2].
C	Information regarding human resource development plans [4.1] is used to support reviews, business decisions, and planning [2.3].
D	Human resource development plans [4.1] derive from and support the organization's overall strategic plans [3.2].
E	Human resource development data [4.1] are analyzed to drive actions to improve employee involvement and recognition [4.2], training [4.3], well-being and satisfaction [4.4], and the development and improvement of front-line customer contact employees [7.2] as needed.
F	Employee-related data [6.3] and organization performance data [6.2] are used to assess the development and well-being of employees, the linkage of human resource practices with key business results, and to ensure that reliable human resource data are available for planning and recruitment.

4.1 Human Resource Planning and Evaluation— Sample Effective Practices

A. Human Resource Plans

- Human resource plans support strategic plans and goals. Plans show how the work force will be developed to enable the organization to achieve its future goals.
- Key issues of training and development, hiring, retention, employee participation, involvement, empowerment, and recognition and reward are addressed.
- Innovative strategies may involve one or more of the following:
  - Redesign of work to increase employee responsibility
  - Improved labor-management relations (that is, prior to contract negotiations, train both sides in effective negotiation skills so that people focus on the merits of issues not positions; improves relations and shortens negotiation time)
  - Forming partnerships with educational institutions to develop employees and ensure a supply of well-prepared future employees
  - Internal customer-supplier partnerships
  - Gainsharing or equity-building compensation systems for all employees
  - Broadening employee responsibilities; creating self-directed or high performance work teams
- Employee skill development goes beyond job requirements.
- Multifaceted reward and recognition systems allow employee recognition of managers and peers.
- Management practices are consistent with quality goals and plans.
- Key performance measures (for example, employee satisfaction or work climate surveys) have been identified to gather data to manage progress. (Note: Improvement results associated with these measures should be reported in 6.3.)

B. Evaluating and Improving Human Resouce Planning and Management

- The effectiveness of human resource planning and alignment with strategic plans is evaluated systematically.
- Data are used to evaluate and improve performance and participation for all types of employees (for example, absenteeism, turnover, grievances, accidents, recognition and reward, and training participation).
- Routine, two-way communication about performance of employees occurs.
- All of the human resource initiatives the organization has put in place to achieve strategic plans are systematically evaluated and improved.

4.2　High Performance Work Systems　(45 Points)

Describe how the company's work and job design and compensation and recognition approaches enable and encourage all employees to contribute effectively to achieving high performance objectives.

Areas to Address:

a.　How the company's work and job design promote high performance. Describe how work and job design: (1) create opportunities for initiative and self-directed responsibility; (2) foster flexibility and rapid response to changing requirements; and (3) ensure effective communications across functions or units that need to work together to meet customer and/or operational requirements.

b.　How the company's compensation and recognition approaches for individuals and groups, including managers, reinforce the effectiveness of the work and job design.

Notes:
(1)　Work design refers to how employees are organized and/or organize themselves in formal and informal, temporary, or longer-term units. This includes work teams, problem-solving teams, functional units, departments, self-managed or managed by supervisors. In some cases, teams might involve individuals in different locations linked via computers or conferencing technology.

Job design refers to responsibilities and tasks assigned to individuals. These responsibilities and tasks help define education and training requirements.

(2)　Examples of approaches to create flexibility [4.2a(2)] in work design might include simplification of job classifications, cross training, job rotation, work layout, and work locations. It might also entail use of technology and changed flow of information to support local decision making.

(3)　Compensation and recognition [4.2b] refer to all aspects of pay and reward, including promotion and bonuses. The company might use a variety of reward and recognition approaches—monetary and nonmonetary, formal and informal, and individual and group.

Compensation and recognition approaches could include profit sharing and compensation based on skill building, use of new skills, and demonstrations of self-learning. The approaches could take into account the linkage to customer retention or other performance objectives.

Employee evaluations and reward and recognition approaches might include peer evaluations, including peers in teams and networks.

This item is scored using the **approach/deployment** scoring guidelines. It emphasizes that high performance requires effective work design and reinforcement.

Area 4.2 calls for information on how job design improves the company's work. The basic aims of such design should be to enable employees to exercise more discretion and decision making, leading to greater flexibility and more rapid response to the changing requirements of the marketplace. Effective job design and flexible work organizations are necessary but may not be sufficient to ensure high performance. Job and organization design needs to be supported by information systems, education, and appropriate training. Such support ensures that information flow supports the job and work designs and that employees possess the skills needed to work in this environment. Also important is effective communication across functions and work units to ensure focus on customer requirements and goal attainment.

Area 4.2b addresses the important alignment of incentives with work systems. The area calls for information on how employee compensation and recognition reinforce high performance job design, work organizations, and teamwork. These are important considerations because there should be a consistency between the company's compensation and recognition system and its work structures and processes. Also, compensation and recognition may need to be based upon demonstrated skills and evaluations by peers in teams and networks.

4.2 High Performance Work Systems

How the company's work and job design and compensation and recognition approaches enable and encourage all employees to contribute effectively to achieving high performance objectives

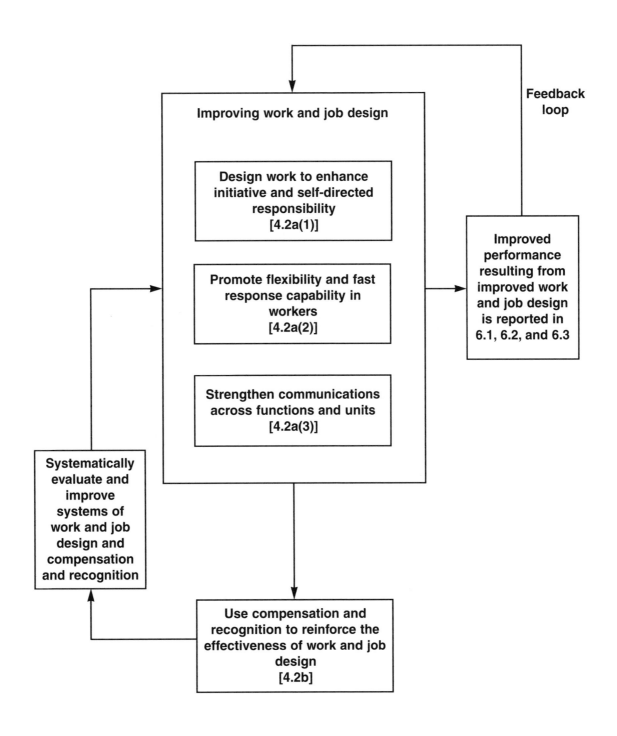

4.2 High Performance Work Systems Item Linkages

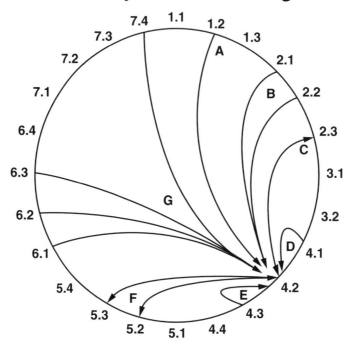

Item	Nature of Relationship
A	Leaders at all levels [1.2 and sometimes 1.1] support efforts to improve employee performance and involvement in quality improvement [4.2].
B	Key benchmarking data [2.2] are used to improve performance systems and reward and recognition [4.2].
C	Information regarding employee involvement and recognition [4.2] is used to gain a better understanding of operational performance and organizational capabilities [2.3a(2)] and to set priorities for improvement actions [2.3b].
D	Human resource development plans [4.1] address ways to improve employee performance and involvement [4.2].
E	Employee performance [4.2] can be enhanced by effective training [4.3].
F	High performance, streamlined work systems [4.2a] and effective recognition [4.2b] are essential to improving operational and support processes [5.2 and 5.3]. Also, the analysis of work processes (identifying inefficiencies) is used to inform or drive the improvements in flexibility and job design.
G	Recognition or rewards [4.2b] are provided based on improvements in product and service quality [6.1], operating effectiveness and financial results [6.2], human resource results [6.3], and customer satisfaction [7.4].

4.2 High Performance Work Systems—Sample Effective Practices

A. Promoting High Performance

- Fully using the talents of all employees is a basic organizational value.
- Managers use cross-functional work teams to break down barriers, improve effectiveness, and meet goals.
- Teams are authorized to take more responsibility for decisions affecting their work.
- Employee opinion is sought regarding work design.
- Prompt and regular feedback is provided to teams regarding their performance. Feedback covers both results and team process.
- Lower scoring organizations use teams for special improvement projects while the regular work is performed using traditional approaches. In higher performing organizations, using teams and self-directed employees is the way regular work is done.
- Self-directed or self-managed work teams are in use throughout the organization. They have authority over matters such as budget, hiring, and team membership and roles.
- A systematic process is used to evaluate and improve the effectiveness and extent of employee involvement.
- Many indicators of employee involvement effectiveness exist, such as the improvements in time or cost reduction produced by teams.
- The organization takes action to improve employee involvement systematically and routinely.

B. Compensation and Recognition Supports Performance

- Recognition and rewards are provided for generating improvement ideas. Also, a system exists to encourage and provide rapid reinforcement for submitting improvement ideas.
- Recognition and rewards are provided for results, such as for reductions in cycle time and exceeding target schedules with error-free products or services at less than projected cost.
- Employees, as well as managers, participate in creating the recognition and rewards system, and they help monitor its implementation and systematic improvement.
- The organization evaluates its approaches to employee performance and recognition and rewards to determine the extent to which employees are satisfied with them, the extent of employee participation, and the impact of the system on improved performance and quality (reported in Item 6.2).
- The results of the evaluation are used to make improvements. Top-scoring organizations have made several improvement cycles. (Many improvement cycles can occur in one year.)

4.3 Employee Education, Training, and Development (50 Points)

Describe how the company's education and training address company plans, including building company capabilities and contributing to employee motivation, progression, and development.

Areas to Address:

a. How the company's education and training serve as a key vehicle in building company and employee capabilities. Describe how education and training address: (1) key performance objectives, including those related to improving customer responsiveness and enhancing high performance work units; and (2) progression and development of all employees.

b. How education and training are designed, delivered, reinforced, evaluated, and improved. Include: (1) how employees and line managers contribute to or are involved in determining specific education and training needs and designing education and training; (2) how education and training are delivered; (3) how knowledge and skills are reinforced through on-the-job application; and (4) how education and training are evaluated and improved.

Notes:

(1) Education and training address the knowledge and skills employees need to meet their overall work objectives. This might include leadership skills, communications, teamwork, problem solving, interpreting and using data, meeting customer requirements, process analysis, process simplification, waste reduction, cycle time reduction, error-proofing, priority setting based upon cost and benefit data, and other training that affects employee effectiveness, efficiency, and safety. It might also include basic skills such as reading, writing, language, and arithmetic.

(2) Training for customer-contact (frontline) employees should address: (a) key knowledge and skills, including knowledge of products and services; (b) listening to customers; (c) soliciting comments from customers; (d) how to anticipate and handle problems or failures ("recovery"); (e) skills in customer retention; and (f) how to manage expectations.

(3) Determining specific education and training needs [4.3b(1)] might include use of company assessment or employee self-assessment to determine and/or compare skill levels for progression within the company or elsewhere. Needs determination should take into account job analysis—the types and levels of skills required—and the timeliness of training.

(4) Education and training delivery [4.3b(2)] might occur inside or outside the company and involve on-the-job, classroom, computer-based, or other types of delivery. This includes the use of developmental assignments within or outside the company to enhance employees' career opportunities and employability.

(5) How education and training are evaluated [4.3b(4)] could address: effectiveness of delivery of education and training; impact on work unit performance; and cost effectiveness of education and training alternatives.

This item is scored using the **approach/deployment** scoring guidelines. It addresses how the company develops the work force via education, training, and on-the-job reinforcement of knowledge and skills. Development is intended to meet the needs of a high performance workplace on an ongoing basis. This means that education and training need to be ongoing as well.

Area 4.3a calls for information on how the company's education and training serve as a key vehicle in building employee capabilities and, therefore, company capabilities. The area focuses on these two capabilities, treating them as investments the company makes in its long-term future and the long-term future of employees.

Area 4.3b calls for information on how education and training are designed, delivered, reinforced, and evaluated, with special emphasis upon on-the-job application of knowledge and skills. The area emphasizes the importance of the involvement of employees and line managers in the design of training, including clear identification of specific needs. This involves job analysis— understanding the types and levels of the skills required and the timeliness of training. The area also emphasizes evaluation of education and training. Such evaluations could take into account line managers' evaluations of value received through education and training relative to needs identified in design. Evaluation could also address the effectiveness of education and training delivery, impact on work unit performance, and cost of delivery alternatives.

4.3 Employee Education, Training, and Development

How the company's education and training address company plans, including building company capabilities and contributing to employee motivation, progression, and development

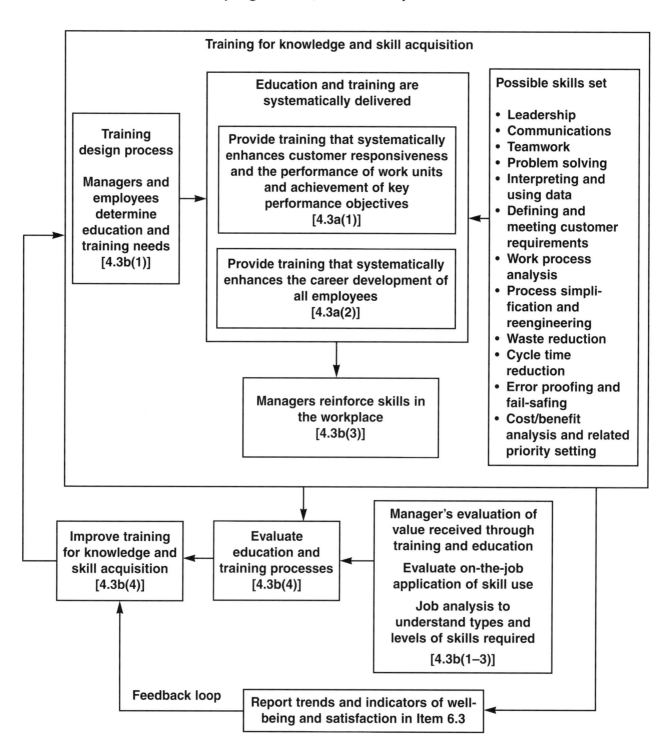

4.3 Employee Education, Training, and Development Item Linkages

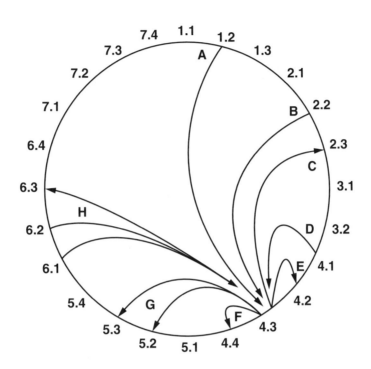

Item	Nature of Relationship
A	Leaders at all levels [1.2 and sometimes 1.1] reinforce training on the job to ensure its effectiveness [4.3].
B	Key measures and benchmarking data [2.2] are used to improve training [4.3].
C	Information regarding training effectiveness and support [4.3] is used to set priorities for improvement actions [2.3b].
D	Human resource development plans [4.1] align training [4.3] to support the organizational goals.
E	Employee performance [4.2] can be enhanced by effective training [4.3].
F	Training [4.3] improves employee flexibility, mobility, and potential [4.4].
G	Training [4.3] is essential to improving work in business processes [5.2 and 5.3].
H	Results of improved training and development [4.3b] are reported in [6.3]. In addition, operational performance results [6.2] and product and service quality results [6.1] are monitored, in part, to assess training effectiveness.

4.3 Employee Education, Training, and Development— Sample Effective Practices

A. Education Assessment and Design

- Systematic needs analyses are conducted by managers and employees to ensure that skills required to perform work are routinely assessed, monitored, and maintained.
- Clear linkages exist between strategic plans and the education and training plans. Skills are developed based on work demands and employee needs.
- Employee input is considered when developing training plans.
- Employee career and personal development options are enhanced through formal education and training, as well as on-the-job training such as rotational assignments or job exchange programs.

B. Education Delivery and Reinforcement

- The organization uses various methods to deliver training to ensure that it is suitable for employee knowledge and skill levels.
- Training is linked to work requirements *that managers reinforce on the job*. Just-in-time training is preferred (rather than just-in-case training) to help ensure that the skills will be used immediately after training.
- Employee feedback on the appropriateness of the training is collected and used to improve the course delivery and content.
- The organization systematically evaluates training effectiveness on the job. Performance data are collected on individuals and groups at all levels to assess the impact of training.
- Employee satisfaction with courses is tracked.
- Training is refined and improved systematically, based on these evaluations.

4.4 Employee Well-Being and Satisfaction (25 Points)

Describe how the company maintains a work environment and a work climate conducive to the well-being and development of all employees.

Areas to Address:

a. How the company maintains a safe and healthful work environment. Include: (1) how employee well-being factors such as health, safety, and ergonomics are included in improvement activities; and (2) principal improvement requirements, measures and/or indicators, and targets for each factor relevant and important to the employees' work environment. Note any significant differences based upon differences in work environments among employees or employee groups.

b. What services, facilities, activities, and opportunities the company makes available to employees to support their overall well-being and satisfaction and/or to enhance their work experience and development potential.

c. How the company determines employee satisfaction, well-being, and motivation. Include a brief description of methods, frequency, the specific factors used in this determination, and how the information is used to improve satisfaction, well-being, and motivation. Note any important differences in methods or factors used for different categories or types of employees, as appropriate.

Notes:

(1) Examples of services, facilities, activities, and opportunities (4.4b) are: personal and career counseling; career development and employability services; recreational or cultural activities; non-work-related education; day care; special leave for family responsibilities and/or for community service; safety off the job; flexible work hours; outplacement; and retiree benefits, including extended health care. These services also might include career enhancement activities such as skill assessment, helping employees develop learning objectives and plans, and employability assessment.

(2) Examples of specific factors which might affect satisfaction, well-being, and motivation are: effective employee problem or grievance resolution; safety; employee views of leadership and management; employee development and career opportunities; employee preparation for changes in technology or work organization; work environment; workload; cooperation and teamwork; recognition; benefits; communications; job security; compensation; equality of opportunity; and capability to provide required services to customers. An effective determination is one that provides the company with actionable information for use in improvement activities.

(3) Measures and/or indicators of satisfaction, well-being, and motivation (4.4c) might include safety, absenteeism, turnover rate for customer-contact employees, grievances, strikes, worker compensation, as well as results of surveys.

(4) How satisfaction, well-being, and motivation information is used (4.4c) might involve developing priorities for addressing employee problems based on impact on productivity.

(5) Trends in key measures and/or indicators of well-being and satisfaction should be reported in Item 6.3.

This item is scored using the **approach/deployment** scoring guidelines. It addresses the work environment and work climate, and how they are tailored to foster the well-being, satisfaction, and development of all employees.

Area 4.4a calls for information regarding a safe and healthful work environment to determine how the company includes such factors in its planning and improvement activities. If different employee groups face different safety or health issues, those differences should be specifically addressed.

Area 4.4b calls for information on the company's approach to enhance employee well-being, satisfaction, and growth potential based upon a holistic view of employees as key stakeholders. The area emphasizes that the company needs to consider a variety of mechanisms to build well-being and satisfaction. Increasingly, these mechanisms relate to development, progression, employability, and external activities. This might include recreational, family, or community service activities.

Area 4.4c calls for information on how the company determines the extent of employee satisfaction, well-being, and motivation. The area recognizes that many factors might affect employee motivation. Although satisfaction with pay and promotion potential is important, these factors may not be adequate to assess the overall climate for motivation and high performance. For this reason, the company may need to consider a variety of factors in the work environment to determine the key factors in motivation. Factors inhibiting motivation need to be prioritized and addressed. Further understanding of these factors could be developed through exit interviews with departing employees.

4.4 Employee Well-Being and Satisfaction

How the company maintains a work environment and a work climate conducive to the well-being and development of all employees

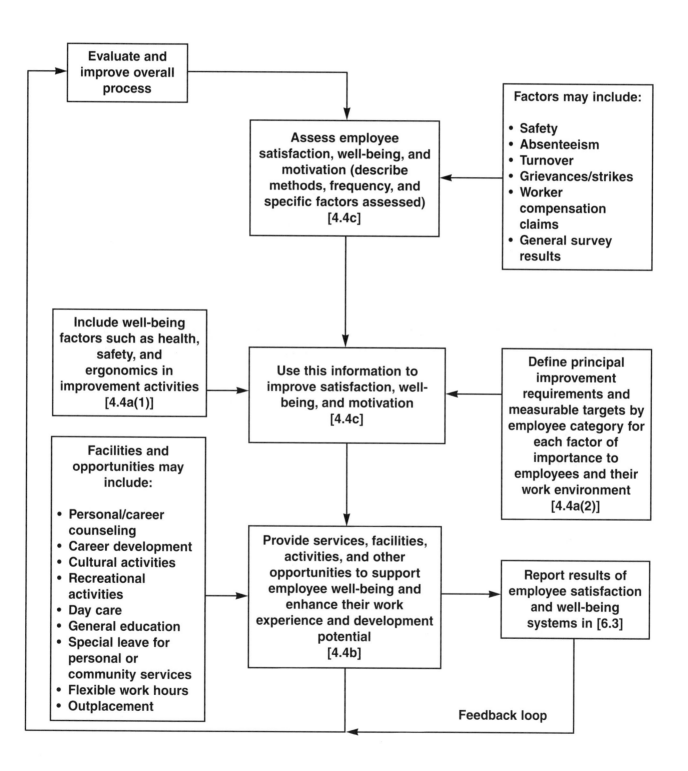

4.4 Employee Well-Being and Satisfaction Item Linkages

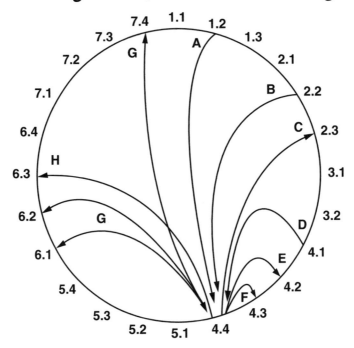

Item	Nature of Relationship
A	Leaders at all levels [1.2 and sometimes 1.1] have responsibility for promoting employee morale and well-being [4.4].
B	Key benchmarking data [2.2] are used to design processes to enhance employee morale and well-being [4.4].
C	Information regarding employee well-being and morale [4.4] is used to set priorities for improvement actions [2.3b].
D	Human resource development plans [4.1] address morale and well-being concerns [4.4].
E	High morale enhances employee involvement [4.2].
F	Training systems [4.3] enhance employee development, flexibility, mobility, and potential [4.4].
G	Systems to enhance employee satisfaction and well-being [4.4] can boost performance [6.1 and 6.2] and customer satisfaction [7.4].
H	Results of employee well-being and satisfaction systems are reported in [6.3].

4.4 Employee Well-Being and Satisfaction—Sample Effective Practices

A. Maintaining a Safe, Healthful Work Environment

- Quality activities consider issues relating to employee health, safety, and workplace environment. Plans exist to optimize these conditions and eliminate adverse conditions.
- Root causes for health and safety problems are systematically identified and eliminated. Corrective actions are communicated widely to help prevent the problem in other parts of the organization.

B. Special Services, Opportunities, Facilities

- Special activities and services are available for employees. These can be quite varied, depending on the needs of employees such as the following:
  - Flexible benefits plan including health care, on-site day care, dental care, portable retirement, education (both work and nonwork related), maternity, paternity, and family illness leave
  - Group purchasing power program where participating merchants are increasing steadily
  - Special facilities for employee meetings to discuss their concerns

C. Determining Employee Satisfaction

- Key employee satisfaction opinion indicators are gathered periodically (usually at least every other year). They may be derived from employee focus groups, E-mail data, employee satisfaction survey results, turnover, absenteeism, stress-related disorders, and other data that reflect employee satisfaction. (A key employee satisfaction indicator is one that reflects conditions affecting employee morale and motivation.)
- On-demand electronic surveys are available for quick response and tabulation any time managers seek employee satisfaction feedback. Managers use the results of these quick-response surveys to focus improvements in work systems and enhance employee satisfaction.

5.0 Process Management—140 Points

The Process Management category examines the key aspects of process management, including customer-focused design, product and service delivery processes, support services, and supply management involving all work units, including research and development. The category examines how key processes are designed, effectively managed, and improved to achieve higher performance.

5.1 Design and Introduction of Products and Services (40 Points)

Describe how new and/or modified products and services are designed and introduced and how key production/delivery processes are designed to meet both key product and service quality requirements, company operational performance requirements, and market requirements.

Areas to Address:

a. How products, services, and production/delivery processes are designed. Describe: (1) how customer requirements are translated into product and service design requirements; (2) how product and service design requirements are translated into efficient and effective production/delivery processes, including an appropriate measurement plan; and (3) how all requirements associated with products, services, and production/delivery processes are addressed early in design by all appropriate company units, suppliers, and partners to ensure integration, coordination, and capability.

b. How product, service, and production/delivery process designs are reviewed and/or tested in detail to ensure a trouble-free and rapid introduction.

c. How designs and design processes are evaluated and improved to achieve better product and service quality, time to market, and production/delivery process effectiveness.

Continued on next page

Notes:
(1) Design and introduction might address:
- *modifications and variants of existing products and services, including product and service customization;*
- *new products and services emerging from research and development or other product/service concept development;*
- *new/modified facilities to meet operational performance and/or product and service requirements; and*
- *significant redesigns or processes to improve customer focus, productivity, or both.*
Design approaches could differ appreciably depending upon the nature of the products/services—entirely new, variants, major or minor process changes, etc. If many design projects are carried out in parallel, responses to Item 5.1 should reflect how coordination of resources among projects is carried out.

(2) Applicants' responses should reflect the key requirements for their products and services. Factors that might need to be considered in design include: health; safety; long-term performance; environmental impact; measurement capability; process capability; manufacturability; maintainability; supplier capability; and documentation.

(3) Service and manufacturing businesses should interpret product and service design requirements to include all product- and service-related requirements at all stages of production, delivery, and use.

(4) A measurement plan [5.1a(2)] should spell out what is to be measured, how and when measurements are to be made, and performance levels or standards to ensure that the results of measurement provide information to guide, monitor, control, or improve the process. This may include service standards used in customer-contact processes. The term, "measurement plan," may also include decisions about key information to collect from customers and/or employees from service encounters, transactions, etc. The actual measurement plan should not be described in Item 5.1. Such information is requested in Item 5.2.

(5) "All appropriate company units" [5.1a(3)] means those units and/or individuals who will take part in production/delivery and whose performance materially affects overall process outcome. This might include groups such as R&D, marketing, design, and product/process engineering.

This item is scored using the **approach/deployment** scoring guidelines. It examines how the company designs and introduces products and services. A major focus of the item is the rapid and effective integration of production and delivery early in the design phase to minimize downstream problems for customers and eliminate the need for design changes that might be costly to the company.

Area 5.1a calls for information on the design of products, services, and their production/delivery processes. Three aspects of this design are examined: (1) the translation of customer requirements into the design requirements for products and services; (2) how the product and service design requirements are translated into efficient and effective production/delivery processes; and (3) how all requirements associated with products, services, and production/delivery processes are addressed early in the design process by all appropriate company units to ensure integration and coordination. Also, many businesses should consider requirements for suppliers and business partners at the design stage. Overall, effective design must take into account all stakeholders in the value chain.

Area 5.1b calls for information on how product, service, and production/delivery process designs are reviewed and tested in detail prior to full-scale launch. Such review and testing is intended to ensure that all parts of the production/delivery system are capable of performing according to design.

Area 5.1c calls for information on how designs and design processes are evaluated and improved to progressively improve quality and cycle time. This area is intended to determine how companies extract lessons learned to build capabilities for future designs. Such evaluation might take into account delays and problems experienced during design, feedback from those involved, and post-launch problems that might have been averted through better design. The evaluation and improvement should strive for a continuous flow of work in the key design and delivery processes.

It should be noted that although the main focus of Item 5.1a is on the design of products, services, and processes to meet customer requirements, effective design must also consider cycle time and productivity of production and delivery processes. This might entail detailed mapping of manufacturing or service processes to achieve efficiency as well as to meet customer requirements.

5.1 Process Management: Design and Introduction of Products and Services

How products, services, and delivery processes are designed to ensure that customer requirements are met

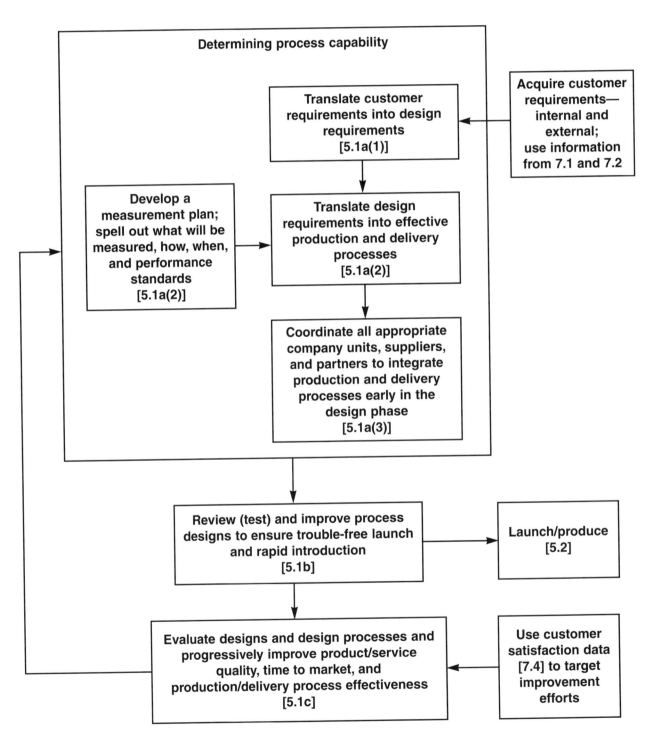

5.1 Design and Introduction of Products and Services Item Linkages

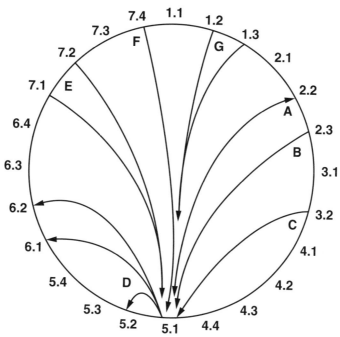

Item	Nature of Relationship
A	Critical work processes [5.1] are used to help identify and prioritize benchmarking targets [2.2]. Benchmarking data [2.2] are used to improve work processes [5.1].
B	Priorities for work process improvements [5.1] are set based on performance data analysis [2.3].
C	Goals, deployed to the work force [3.2], are used to drive and align actions to achieve improved performance [5.1].
D	Processes to ensure products and services are designed to meet customer requirements and have a trouble-free launch [5.1] affect product and service production and delivery [5.2], product and service quality [6.1], and operating performance and financial results [6.2].
E	Information about customer requirements [7.1] and information from customers' hot lines (complaints) through customer contact employees [7.2] is used to design products and services [5.1].
F	Information about customer satisfaction [7.4] is used to target improvement efforts in product and service design and development processes [5.1].
G	Managers at all levels [1.2] have a responsibility for ensuring work processes are designed [5.1], to be consistent with organizational objectives, including those relating to public responsibility and corporate citizenship.

5.1 Design and introduction of Products and Services

A. Translating Customer Requirements into Product and Service Designs

- A systematic iterative process (for example, quality function deployment) is used to maintain a focus on customer requirements and to convert customer requirements into product or service design, production, and delivery.
- Product design requirements are systematically translated into process specifications with measurement plans to monitor the process.
- The work of various functions is coordinated to bring the product or service through the design-to-delivery phases. Functional barriers between units have been eliminated organization-wide.
- Concurrent engineering is used to operate several processes (for example, product and service planning, research and development, manufacturing, marketing, supplier certification) in parallel as much as possible, rather than operating in sequence. All activities are closely coordinated through effective communication and teamwork.

B. Reviewing and Validating the Design Process

- Internal process capacity and supplier capability using measures such as Cpk are reviewed and considered before production and delivery process designs or plans are finalized.
- Market, design, production, service, and delivery reviews occur at defined intervals or as needed.
- Steps are taken (such as design testing or prototyping) to ensure that the production and delivery process will work as designed and will meet customer requirements.

C. Evaluating and Improving the Design Process

- Design processes are evaluated.
- Improvements have been made so future designs are developed faster (shorter cycle time), at lower cost, and with higher quality relative to key product or service characteristics that predict customer satisfaction.
- The results of improved design process performance are reported in 6.2.

5.2 Process Management: Product and Service Production and Delivery (40 Points)

Describe how the company's key product and service production/delivery processes are managed to ensure that design requirements are met and that both quality and operational performance are continuously improved.

Areas to Address:

a. How the company maintains the performance of key production/delivery processes to ensure that such processes meet design requirements addressed in Item 5.1. Describe: (1) the key processes and their principal requirements; and (2) the measurement plan and how measurements and/or observations are used to maintain process performance.

b. How processes are evaluated and improved to improve products and services and to achieve better operational performance, including cycle time. Describe how each of the following is used or considered: (1) process analysis and research; (2) benchmarking; (3) use of alternative technology; and (4) information from customers of the processes—within and outside the company.

Notes:

(1) Key production/delivery processes are those most directly involved in fulfilling the principal requirements of customers—those that define the products and services.

(2) Measurement plan [5.2a(2)] is defined in Item 5.1, Note (4). Companies with specialized measurement requirements should describe how they ensure measurement effectiveness. For specialized physical, chemical, and engineering measurements, describe briefly how measurements are made traceable to national standards.

(3) The focus of 5.2a is on maintenance of process performance using measurements and/or observations to decide whether or not corrective action is needed. The nature of the corrective action depends on the process characteristics and the type of variation observed. Responses should reflect the type of process and the type of variation observed. A description should be given of how basic (root) causes of variation are determined and how corrections are made at the earliest point(s) in processes. Such correction should then minimize the likelihood of recurrence of this type of variation anywhere in the company.

(4) The focus of 5.2b is on improvement of processes—making them perform better than the original design. Better performance might include one or more of the following: operational, customer-related, and financial performance. After processes have been improved, process maintenance (5.2a) needs to adjust to the changes. Process improvement methods might utilize financial data to evaluate alternatives and set priorities.

Continued on next page

(5) Process analysis and research [5.2b(1)] refers to a wide range of possible approaches to improving processes. Examples include process mapping, optimization experiments, basic and applied research, error proofing, and reviewing critical encounters between employees and customers from the point of view of customers and employees.

(6) Information from customers [5.2b(4)] might include information developed as described in Items 7.2, 7.3, and 2.3.

(7) Results of improvements in products and services and in product and service delivery processes should be reported in Items 6.1 and 6.2, as appropriate.

This item is scored using the **approach/deployment** scoring guidelines. It addresses two different but related concerns—how the company maintains key production and delivery processes, and how it improves them.

Area 5.2a calls for information on the maintenance of process performance to ensure that processes consistently perform according to their design. The information required includes a description of the key processes and their specific requirements, and how performance relative to these requirements is known and maintained. Specific reference is made to a measurement plan. A measurement is followed to identify critical points in processes for measurements or observation. Measurements or observations are made at the earliest points in processes to minimize problems that may result from variations from expected (design) performance. When measurements or observations reveal such variations, a remedy—usually called a corrective action—is put in place to restore the actual performance of the process to its design performance. Depending on the nature of the process, the correction could involve technical, human, or other factors. Proper correction involves correcting the problem at the source (root cause) of the variation. In some cases, customers may directly witness or take part in the process, and contribute to or be a determinant of process performance. In such cases, variations among customers must be taken into account in evaluating how well the process is performing. This might entail specific or general contingencies, depending on customer response. This is especially true of professional and personal services.

Area 5.2b calls for information on how processes are improved to achieve better performance. Better performance means not only better quality from the customer's perspective but also better operational performance—such as productivity—from the company's perspective. Area 5.2b anticipates that companies use a variety of process improvement approaches. Area 5.2b calls for information on how the company uses or considers four key approaches: process mapping, benchmarking, technology, and information from the customers of the process.

5.2 Process Management: Product and Service Production and Delivery

How the company's key product and service production/delivery processes are managed to ensure that design requirements are met and that both quality and operational performance are continuously improved

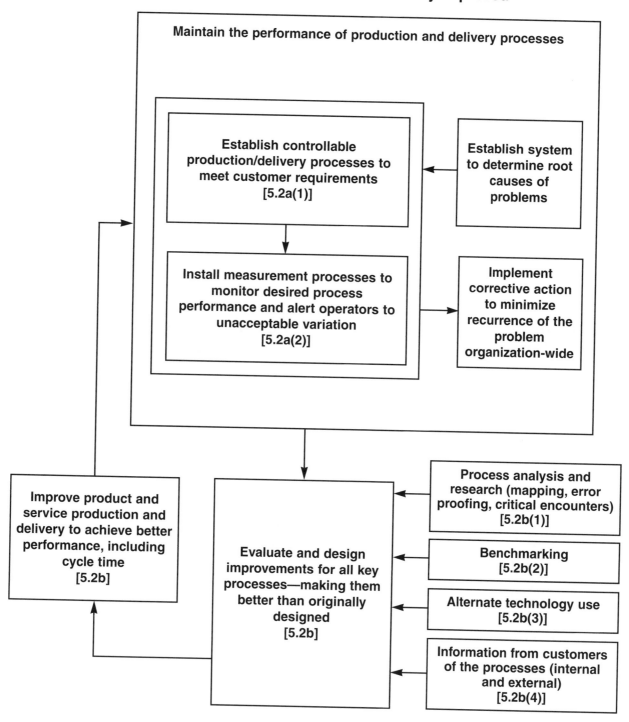

5.2 Process Management: Product and Service Production and Delivery Item Linkages

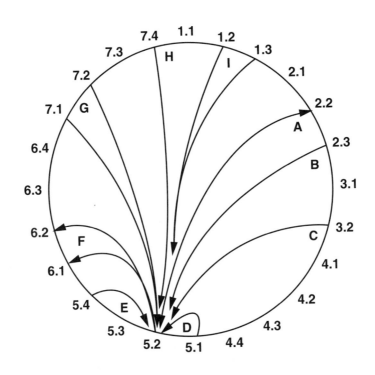

Item	Nature of Relationship
A	Critical work processes [5.2] are used to help identify and prioritize benchmarking targets [2.2]. Benchmark data [2.2] are used to improve work processes [5.2].
B	Priorities for process improvement [5.2] are set based on performance data analysis [2.3].
C	Stretch goals [3.2] are used to drive key process improvements [5.2].
D	Processes to ensure products and services are designed to meet customer requirements and have trouble-free launches [5.1] enhance product and service production and delivery [5.2].
E	Improved supplier processes [5.4] may be required to improve work processes [5.2].
F	Improved work processes [5.2] produce better results [6.1 and 6.2] or at least eliminate problems that disrupt work processes.
G	Information about customer requirements [7.1] and customer relations [7.2] is used to identify improvement opportunities in operating work processes [5.2].
H	Information about customer satisfaction [7.4] is used to target improvement efforts in operating work processes [5.2].
I	Managers [1.2] ensure work processes are aligned with organization priorities [5.2] including regulatory and public responsibilities [1.3].

Note: Human resource capabilities [4.2, 4.3, 4.4] also impact work process efficiency [5.2].

5.2 Process Management: Product and Service Production and Delivery—Sample Effective Practices

A. Maintaining Production/Delivery Performance

- Performance requirements (from Item 5.1, design processes and customer requirements) are set using facts and data, such as statistical process control.
- Production and service delivery processes are measured and tracked. Measures (quantitative and qualitative) should reflect or assess the extent to which customer requirements are met.
- For processes that produce defects (out-of-control processes), root causes are systematically identified and corrective action is taken to prevent their recurrence.
- Corrections are monitored and verified. Processes used and results obtained should be systematic and integrated throughout the organization.

B. Evaluating and Improving Operational Processes

- Processes are systematically reviewed to improve productivity, reduce cycle time and waste, and increase quality.
- Work process simplification or improvement tools are used, such as flowcharting, work redesign, and reengineering.
- Benchmarking, competitive comparison data, and information from customers of the process (in or out of the organization) are used to gain insight to improve processes.

5.3 Process Management: Support Services (30 Points)

Describe how the company's key support service processes are designed and managed so that current requirements are met and operational performance is continuously improved.

Areas to Address:

a. How key support processes are designed. Include: (1) how key requirements are determined or set; (2) how these requirements are translated into efficient and effective processes, including operational requirements and an appropriate measurement plan; and (3) how all requirements are addressed early in design by all appropriate company units to ensure integration, coordination, and capability.

b. How the company maintains the performance of key support service processes to ensure that such processes meet design requirements. Describe: (1) the key processes and their principal requirements; and (2) the measurement plan and how measurements are used to maintain process performance.

c. How processes are evaluated and improved to achieve better performance, including cycle time. Describe how each of the following is used or considered: (1) process analysis and research; (2) benchmarking; (3) use of alternative technology; and (4) information from customers of the processes—within and outside the company.

Notes:
(1) Support services are those that support the company's product and/or service delivery but that are not usually designed in detail with the products and services themselves because their requirements do not usually depend a great deal upon product and service characteristics. Support service design requirements usually depend significantly upon internal requirements. Support services might include finance and accounting, software services, sales, marketing, public relations, information services, supplies, personnel, legal services, plant and facilities management, research and development, and secretarial and other administrative services.

Continued on next page

(2) The purpose of Item 5.3 is to permit applicants to highlight separately the design (5.3a), maintenance (5.3b), and improvement (5.3c) activities for processes that support the product and service design, production, and delivery processes addressed in Items 5.1 and 5.2. The support service processes included in Item 5.3 depend on the applicant's type of business and other factors. Thus, this selection should be made by the applicant. Together, Items 5.1, 5.2, 5.3, and 5.4 should cover all key operations, processes, and activities of all work units.

(3) Measurement plan [5.3a(2)] is described in Item 5.1, Note (4). Process maintenance [5.3b] is described in Item 5.2, Note (3). Process improvement [5.3c] is described in Item 5.2, Note (4).

(4) "Process analysis and research" [5.3c(1)] refers to a wide range of possible approaches to improving processes. See Item 5.2, Note (5).

(5) Information from customers [5.3c(4)] might include information developed as described in Items 7.2, 7.3, and 2.3. However, most of the information for improvement [5.3c(4)] is likely to come from "internal customers"—those within the company who use the support services.

(6) Results of improvements in support services should be reported in 6.2.

This item is scored using the **approach/deployment** scoring guidelines. It addresses how the company designs, maintains, and improves its support service processes.

Area 5.3a calls for information on the design of key support service processes. Such design should be based upon the requirements of the company's (internal) customers—those units and workers within the company who use the output of the support process. The requirements of effective design are, as required for operational processes in Item 5.1, coordinated and integrated to ensure efficient and effective performance.

Area 5.3b calls for information on how the company maintains the performance of the key support service processes. This information includes a description of the key control processes and their principal requirements and a description of the measurement plan and how it is used. The requirements of Area 5.3b are similar to those described above in Area 5.2a.

Area 5.3c calls for information on how the company evaluates and improves the performance of the key support service processes. The area calls for information on how the company uses or considers the same four key approaches described in 5.2c.

5.3 Process Management: Support Services

How the company's key support service processes are designed and managed so that current requirements are met and that operational performance is continuously improved

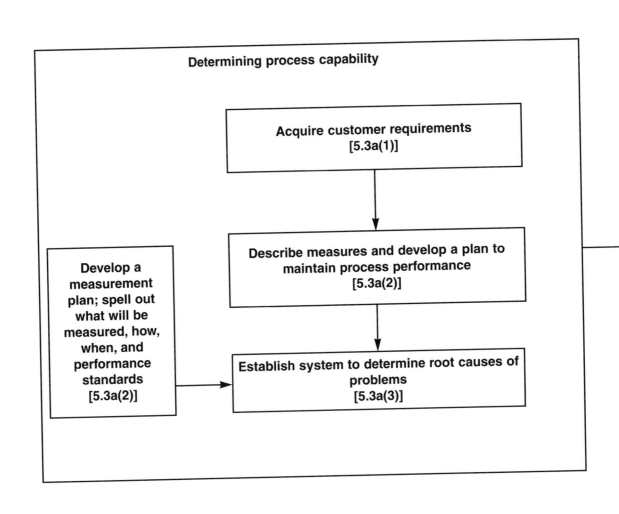

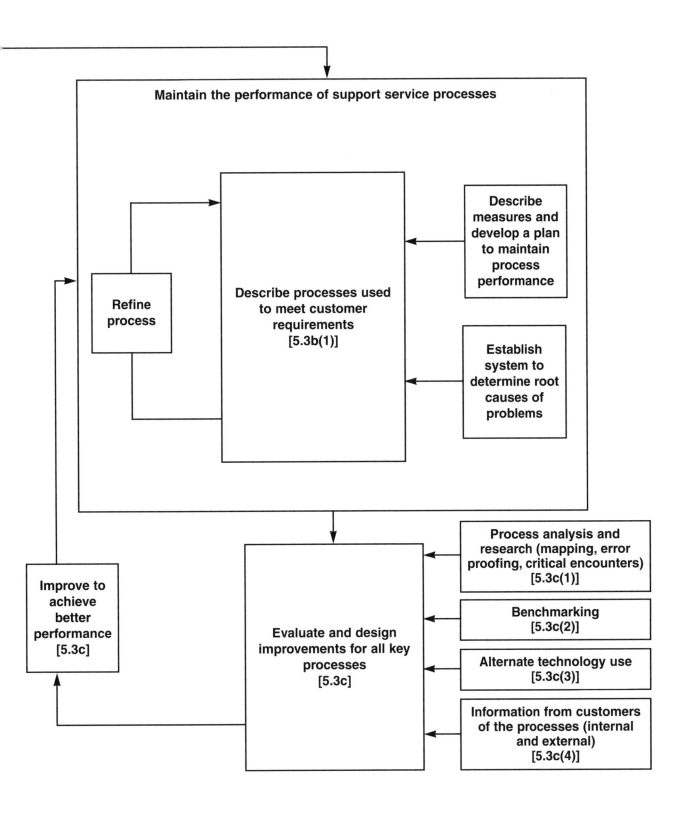

5.3 Process Management: Support Services Item Linkages

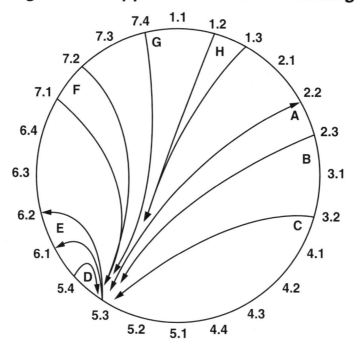

Item	Nature of Relationship
A	Critical work processes in the support area [5.3] are used to help identify and prioritize benchmarking targets [2.2]. Benchmarking data [2.2] are used to improve support work processes [5.3].
B	Priorities for support work processes improvement [5.3] are set based on performance data and analysis [2.3].
C	Goals [3.2], deployed to the work force, are used to drive and align actions to achieve improved support performance [5.3].
D	Improved supplier performance [5.4] may be required to improve support work processes [5.3].
E	Improved support work processes [5.3] produce better product and service quality and operational and financial results [6.1 and 6.2].
F	Information about customer requirements [7.1] and from customer relations personnel [7.2] is used to identify improvement opportunities in support work processes [5.3].
G	Information about customer satisfaction [7.4] is used to target improvement efforts in support work processes [5.3].
H	Managers [1.2] ensure support processes are aligned with organization priorities [5.2] including regulatory and public responsibilities [1.3].

Note: Human resource capabilities [4.2, 4.3, 4.4] also impact work process efficiency [5.2].

5.3 Process Management: Support Services— Sample Effective Practices

A. Designing Support Service

- A formal process exists to understand internal customer requirements, translate those requirements into efficient service processes, and measure their effectiveness.
- Specific improvements in support services are made with the same rigor as improvements in operating processes.
- All support services are subject to continuous review and improvements in performance and customer satisfaction.

B. Maintaining Business Support Service Performance

- Systems to ensure process performance are maintained and customer requirements are met.
- Root causes of problems are systematically identified and corrected for processes that produce defects.
- Corrections are monitored and verified. Processes used and results obtained should be systematic and integrated throughout the organization.

C. Evaluating and Improving Processes

- Support processes are systematically reviewed to improve productivity, reduce cycle time and waste, and increase quality.
- Work process simplification or improvement tools are used.
- Stretch goals are used to drive higher levels of performance.
- Benchmarking, competitive comparison data, or information from customers of the process (in or out of the organization) are used to gain insight to improve processes.

5.4 *Management of Supplier Performance (30 Points)*

Describe how the company assures that materials, components, and services furnished by other businesses meet the company's performance requirements. Describe also the company's actions and plans to improve supplier relationships and performance.

Areas to Address:

a. Summary of the company's requirements and how they are communicated to suppliers. Include: (1) a brief summary of the principal requirements for key suppliers, the measures and/or indicators associated with these requirements, and the expected performance levels; (2) how the company determines whether or not its requirements are met by suppliers; and (3) how performance information is fed back to suppliers.

b. How the company evaluates and improves its management of supplier relationships and performance. Describe current actions and plans: (1) to improve suppliers' abilities to meet requirements; (2) to improve the company's own procurement processes, including feedback sought from suppliers and from other units within the company ("internal customers") and how such feedback is used; and (3) to minimize costs associated with inspection, test, audit, or other approaches used to track and verify supplier performance.

Notes:

(1) The term "supplier" refers to other-company providers of goods and services. The use of these goods and services may occur at any stage in the production, design, delivery, and use of the company's products and services. Thus, suppliers include businesses such as distributors, dealers, warranty repair services, transportation, contractors, and franchises as well as those that provide materials and components.

   If the applicant is a unit of a larger company, and other units of that company supply goods/services, this should be included as part of Item 5.4.

   The term "supplier" also refers to service suppliers such as health care, training, and education.

(2) Key suppliers [5.4a(1)] are those that provide the most important products and/or services, taking into account the criticality and volume of products and/or services involved.

(3) "Requirements" refers to the principal factors involved in the purchases; quality, delivery, and price.

Continued on next page

(4) How requirements are communicated and how performance information is fed back might entail ongoing working relationships or partnerships with key suppliers. Such relationships and/or partnerships should be briefly described in responses.

(5) Processes for determining whether or not requirements are met [5.4a(2)] might include audits, process reviews, receiving inspection, certification, testing, and rating systems.

(6) Actions and plans (5.4b) might include one or more of the following: joint planning, rapid information and data exchanges, use of benchmarking and comparative information, customer-supplier teams, partnerships, training, long-term agreements, incentives, and recognition. Actions and plans might also include changes in supplier selection, leading to a reduction in the number of suppliers.

(7) Efforts to minimize costs might be backed by analyses comparing suppliers based on overall cost, taking into account quality and delivery. Analyses might also address transaction costs associated with alternative approaches to supply management.

This item is scored using the **approach/deployment** scoring guidelines. It addresses how the company manages performance of external providers of goods and services. Such management might be built around longer-term partnering relationships, particularly with key suppliers.

Area 5.4a calls for basic information on the company's principal requirements for its key suppliers, expected performance and measures used to assess performance, how the company determines whether or not its requirements are being met, and how performance information is fed back to suppliers.

Area 5.4b calls for information on how the company evaluates and improves its supplier management. This includes three main elements: improving supplier abilities to meet requirements; improving its own supplier management processes; and reducing costs associated with the verification of supplier performance.

For many companies, suppliers are an increasingly important part of achieving not only high performance and lower-cost objectives, but also strategic objectives. For example, key suppliers might provide unique design, integration, and marketing capabilities. Exploiting these advantages requires joint planning and partner relationships. Such planning and relationship building might entail the use of longer-term planning horizons and customer-supplier teams.

5.4 Management of Supplier Performance

How the company ensures that materials, components, and services furnished by other businesses meet the company's performance requirements

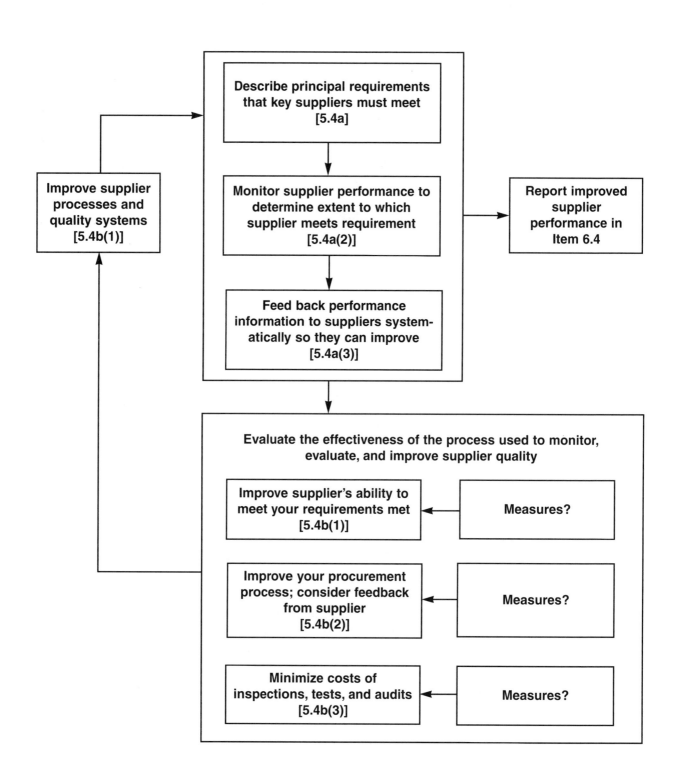

5.4 Management of Supplier Performance Item Linkages

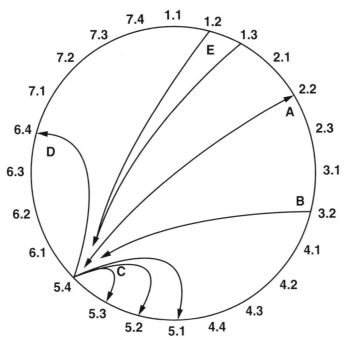

Item	Nature of Relationship
A	Issues in supplier improvement processes [5.4] are used to help identify and prioritize benchmarking targets [2.2]. Benchmarking data [2.2] are used to improve supplier performance initiatives [5.4].
B	Stretch goals [3.2], deployed through the key supplier chain, are used to drive improved supplier performance [5.4] in critical areas.
C	Improved supplier performance [5.4] may be required to improve work processes [5.1, 5.2, and 5.3].
D	Improved supplier processes [5.4] result in better supplier performance [6.4].
E	Managers at all levels [1.2] who interact with suppliers have a responsibility to ensure systematic improvement of supplier performance on key quality indicators [5.4] and ensure that suppliers do not act in a manner inconsistent with the organization's commitment to the public, including regulatory compliance [1.3].

5.4 Management of Supplier Performance—Sample Effective Practices

A. Communicating Quality Requirements

- Quality requirements are clearly defined and communicated to suppliers.
- Decisions on which suppliers to use are driven by measurable quality characteristics of the supplier, rather than price alone.
- Measures of expected supplier performance are in place.
- Data on supplier performance are provided to suppliers.

B. Evaluating and Improving Supplier Relationships and Performance

- The organization has a system in place to review and improve its own procurement processes and processes for communicating with and selecting suppliers.
- Procedures are in place to improve supplier quality (for example, fewer defective parts, less rework and scrap, faster response time) that may include supplier training or certification programs.
- Actions are taken to reduce unnecessary costs such as incoming inspection or testing by improving the internal performance systems of suppliers.

6.0 Business Results—250 Points

The Business Results category examines the company's performance and improvement in key business areas—product and service quality, productivity and operational effectiveness, supply quality, and financial performance indicators linked to these areas. Also examined are performance levels relative to competitors.

6.1 Product and Service Quality Results (75 Points)

Summarize performance results for products and services and/or product and service offerings and results of improvement efforts, using key measures and/or indicators of such performance and improvement.

Areas to Address:

a. Current levels and trends in key measures and/or indicators of quality of products and services and/or product and service offerings. Graphs and tables should include appropriate comparative data.

Notes:

(1) Results reported in Item 6.1 should reflect performance relative to key specific non-price product and service requirements—those described in the Business Overview and addressed in Items 7.1, 3.1, and 5.1. The measures and/or indicators should address factors that affect customer preference—performance, timeliness, availability, and variety. Examples include defect levels, repeat services, delivery response times, and complaint levels.

(2) Data appropriate for inclusion might be based upon one or more of the following:
- *internal (company) measurements;*
- *field performance;*
- *data collected by the company or on behalf of the company through follow-ups (7.2c) or surveys of customers on product and service performance; and*
- *data collected or generated by other organizations, including customers.*

Although data appropriate for inclusion are primarily based upon internal measurements and field performance, data collected by the company or other organizations through follow-ups might be included for attributes that cannot be accurately assessed through direct measurement (e.g., ease of use) or when variability in customer expectations makes the customer's perception the most meaningful indicator (e.g., courtesy).

(3) Comparative data might include industry best, best competitor, industry average, and appropriate benchmarks. Such data might be derived from independent surveys, studies, laboratory testing, or other sources.

This item is scored using the **results** scoring guidelines. It addresses current levels and trends in product and service quality using key measures and/or indicators of such quality. The measures or indicators selected should relate to requirements that matter to the customer and to the marketplace. These features are derived from customer-related items ("listening posts") that make up Category 7.0. These data are collected from within-company sources since they are measures of product and service characteristics, not customer satisfaction.

If the features have been properly selected, improvements in them should show strong positive correlation with customer and marketplace improvement indicators, which are captured in Item 7.4. The correlation between quality and customer indicators is a critical management tool—a device for focusing on key quality requirements. In addition, the correlation may reveal emerging or changing market segments, changing importance of requirements, or even potential obsolescence of products and services.

Area 6.1a calls for data on current levels and trends in product and service quality. The area also calls for comparative information so that the results reported can be evaluated against competitors or other relevant markers of performance.

6.1 Product and Service Quality Results

Results of improvement efforts using key measures and/or indicators of product and service quality

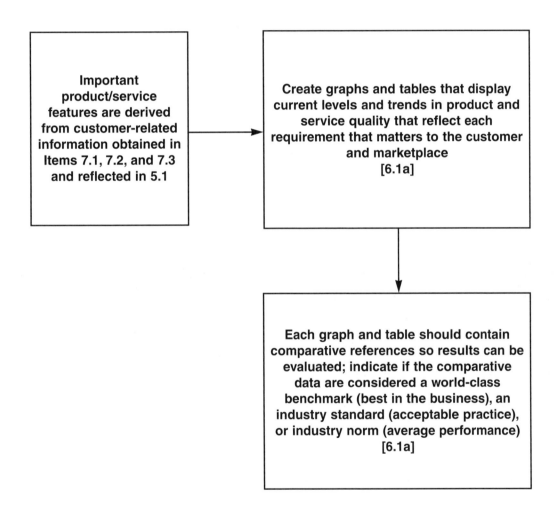

Important product/service features are derived from customer-related information obtained in Items 7.1, 7.2, and 7.3 and reflected in 5.1

Create graphs and tables that display current levels and trends in product and service quality that reflect each requirement that matters to the customer and marketplace
[6.1a]

Each graph and table should contain comparative references so results can be evaluated; indicate if the comparative data are considered a world-class benchmark (best in the business), an industry standard (acceptable practice), or industry norm (average performance)
[6.1a]

Note: If product/service quality features have been correctly identified, there should be a strong positive correlation between 6.1 results and the results in 7.4.

6.1 Product and Service Quality Results Item Linkages

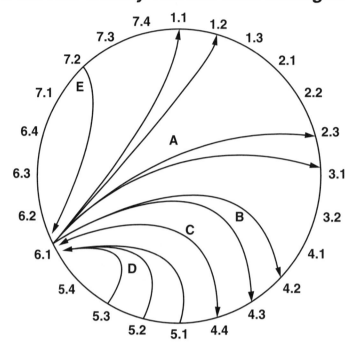

Item	Nature of Relationship
A	Product and service quality characteristics results data (which reflect the extent to which customer requirements were met) are collected and used for planning, management, decision making, and priority setting. See descriptions of leadership [1.0], information and analysis [2.0], strategy development, [3.0] recognition and reward, [4.2b] and training effectiveness [4.3].
B	Employee morale and well-being [4.4] affect product and service quality results [6.1] and vice versa.
C	Designing products and services to meet customer requirements [5.1], improved operational performance [5.2], and support performance [5.3] affects product and service quality [6.1].
D	Customer relations systems [7.2] result in improved complaint response time, effective complaint resolution, and percent of complaints resolved on first contact. These results should be reported in 6.1.

6.1 Product and Service Quality Results—Sample Effective Practices

A. Trends and Current Levels for Key Product/Service Measures

- Quality indices and trend data (three-year minimum preferred) are provided in graph and chart form for all product and service measures identified in 5.1, 2.1, relevant organizational goals (3.2), and the key business factors identified in the business overview.
- All indicators show steady improvement.
- Graphs and information are clear and easy to understand.
- Results data reflect performance relative to specific nonprice product and service key quality requirements that relate closely to customer satisfaction and customer retention.
- Product and service quality measures and indicators address requirements such as accuracy, timeliness, and reliability, and are key to predicting customer behavior. Examples include defect levels, repeat services, meeting product or service delivery or response times, availability levels, and complaint levels.
- Comparative data include industry best, best competitor, industry average, and appropriate benchmarks. Data are also derived from independent surveys, studies, laboratory testing, or other sources.
- Data are not missing. (For example, do not show a steady trend from 1990 to 1994, but leave out 1992.)
- Quality results of competitors, benchmarks, industry leaders, or world-class providers are presented as appropriate.
- Data are not aggregated since aggregation tends to hide poor performance by blending it with good performance. Break out and report trends separately.

6.2 Company Operational and Financial Results (110 Points)

Summarize results of the company's operational and financial performance and performance improvement efforts using key measures and/or indicators of such performance and improvement.

Areas to Address:

a. Current levels and trends in key measures and/or indicators of company operational and financial performance. Graphs and tables should include appropriate comparative data.

Notes:

(1) Key measures and/or indicators of company operational and financial performance include the following areas:

- *productivity and other indicators of effective use of manpower, materials, energy, capital, and assets. (Aggregate measures such as total factor productivity, ROI, margin rates, operating profit rates, and working capital productivity are encouraged. Aggregate economic and/or market value measures are also appropriate.);*
- *company-specific indicators such as innovation rates, innovation effectiveness, cost reductions through innovation, and time to market;*
- *environmental improvements reflected in emissions levels, waste stream reductions, by-product use and recycling, etc. (See Item 1.3);*
- *cycle time, lead times, set-up times, and other responsiveness indicators; and*
- *process assessment results such as customer assessment or third-party assessment (such as ISO 9000).*

(2) Comparative data might include industry best, best competitor, industry average, and appropriate benchmarks.

This item is scored using the **results** scoring guidelines. It addresses the operational and financial performance of the company. Paralleling Item 6.1, which focuses on requirements that matter to the customer, Item 6.2 focuses on factors that best reflect overall company operational performance. Such factors are of two types: (1) generic, common to all companies; and (2) business-specific. Generic factors include financial indicators, cycle time, and productivity, as reflected in use of labor, materials, energy, capital, and assets. Generic factors also include human resource indicators such as safety, absenteeism, and turnover. Productivity, cycle time, or other operational indicators should reflect aggregate company performance. Business- or company-specific effectiveness indicators vary greatly. Examples include rates of invention or patent filing, environmental quality, export levels, new markets, percent of sales from recently introduced products or services, and shifts toward new segments.

Area 6.2a calls for data on current levels and trends in company operational and financial performance. The area also calls for comparative information so that results reported can be evaluated against competitors or other relevant markers of performance.

6.2 Company Operational and Financial Results

Results of improvement efforts using key measures and/or indicators of company operational and financial performance

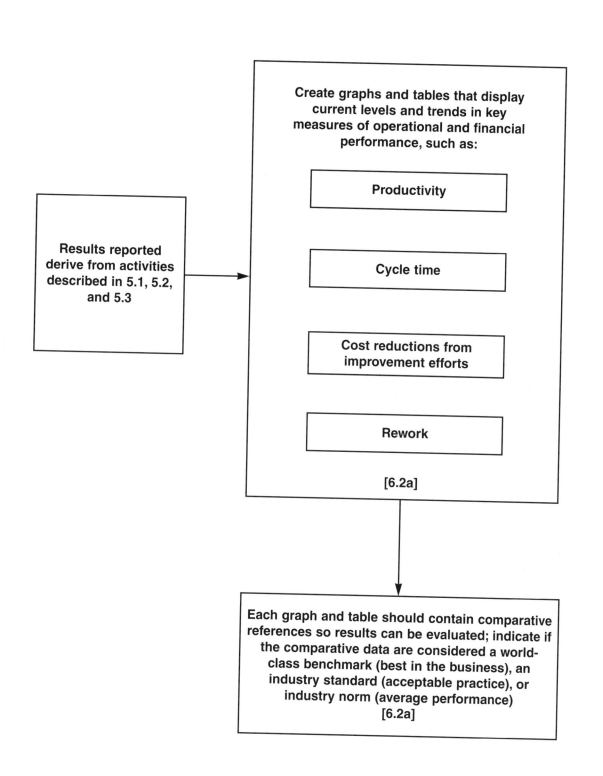

Results reported derive from activities described in 5.1, 5.2, and 5.3

Create graphs and tables that display current levels and trends in key measures of operational and financial performance, such as:

Productivity

Cycle time

Cost reductions from improvement efforts

Rework

[6.2a]

Each graph and table should contain comparative references so results can be evaluated; indicate if the comparative data are considered a world-class benchmark (best in the business), an industry standard (acceptable practice), or industry norm (average performance)
[6.2a]

6.2 Company Operational and Financial Results Item Linkages

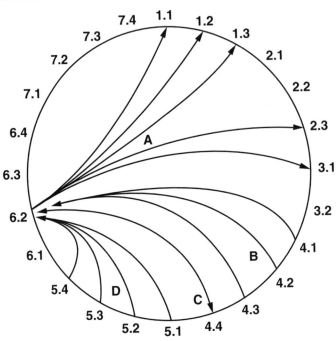

Item	Nature of Relationship
A	Operational performance results data [6.2] are collected and used for planning [3.1], management monitoring and decision making [1.1 and 1.2], and priority setting [2.3]. Key results in areas of public responsibility are monitored to ensure compliance with public safety and other regulatory requirements [1.3].
B	Employee morale and well-being [4.4] affect operational performance results [6.2] and vice versa.
C	Operational results [6.2] are enhanced by improvements in design and development [5.1], operational processes [5.2], support processes [5.3] and supplier effectiveness [5.4].

6.2 Company Operational and Financial Results— Sample Effective Practices

A. Trends and Current Levels for Operational Results

Note: Operational performance measures address productivity, efficiency and effectiveness such as productivity indices, human resource utilization, waste reduction, energy efficiency, cycle time reduction, and product/service design improvement measures.

- Quality indices and trend data (three-year minimum preferred) are provided (graph and chart form) for all performance measures identified in 5.2 and 2.1, and relative operational goals in 3.2.
- All indicators show steady improvement.
- Graphs and information are clear and easy to understand.
- Data are not missing.
- Key measures and indicators of organization operational and financial performance address the following areas:
  - Productivity and other indicators of effective use of materials, energy, capital, and assets
  - Cycle time and responsiveness
  - Financial indicators such as cost reductions, asset utilization, and benefit/cost results from improvement efforts
  - Safety, absenteeism, turnover, and satisfaction
  - Public responsibilities such as environmental improvements
  - Organization-specific indicators such as innovation rates and progress in shifting markets or segments
- Comparative data include industry best, best competitor, industry average, and appropriate benchmarks. For human resource areas such as turnover or absenteeism, local or regional comparative information is used as appropriate.
- Report data for each logical measure. For example, if three product lines exist, report operational results separately—do not aggregate into one trend line.

6.3 Human Resource Results (35 Points)

Summarize human resource results, including employee development and indicators of employee well-being and satisfaction.

Areas to Address:

a. Current levels and trends in key measures and/or indicators of employee development, well-being, satisfaction, self-directed responsibility, and effectiveness. Graphs and tables should include appropriate comparative data.

Notes:

(1) Measures and/or indicators should include safety, absenteeism, turnover, and satisfaction. Comparative data might include industry best, best competitors, industry average, and appropriate benchmarks. Local or regional data on absenteeism and turnover are also appropriate. Financial measures such as worker compensation cost or turnover cost reductions are appropriate for inclusion.

(2) Measures and/or indicators of development should cover not only extent (for example, percent of employees trained or hours of training per year) but also effectiveness. Financial information such as benefit cost ratios for training is appropriate for inclusion.

(3) Examples of satisfaction factors are given in Item 4.4, Note (2).

(4) The results reported in Item 6.3 derive from activities described in the Items of Category 4.0. Results should address all categories and types of employees.

This item is scored using the **results** scoring guidelines. It addresses the company's human resource results—those relating to employee development, effectiveness, well-being, and satisfaction.

Results reported could include generic and business- or company-specific factors. Generic factors include safety, absenteeism, turnover, and satisfaction. Business- or company-specific factors include those commonly used in the industry or created by the company for purposes of tracking progress. Results reported might include input data, such as extent of training, but the main emphasis should be placed on measures of effectiveness.

Area 6.3a calls for data on current levels and trends in key human resource areas—development, well-being, satisfaction, self-directed responsibility, and effectiveness. The area also calls for comparative information so that results can be meaningfully evaluated against competitors or other relevant external measures of performance.

6.3 Human Resource Results

Results of supplier performance improvement efforts using key measures and/or indicators of such performance

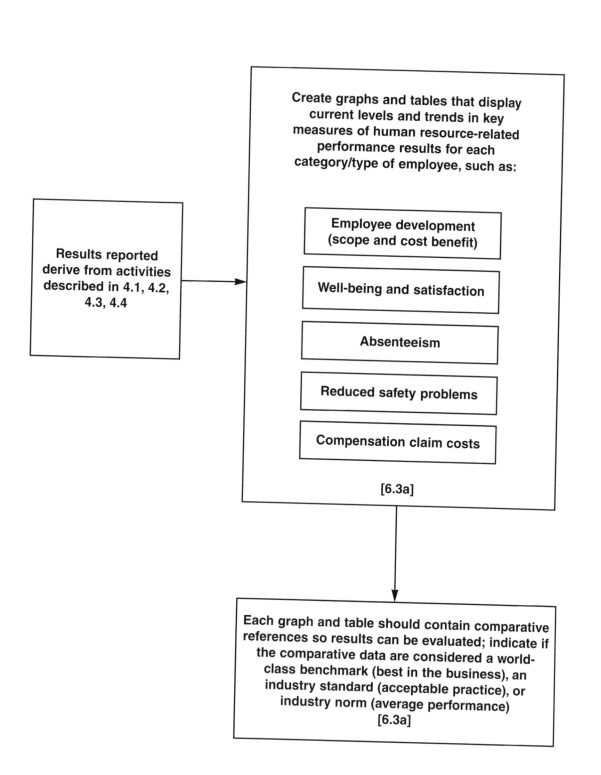

Results reported derive from activities described in 4.1, 4.2, 4.3, 4.4

Create graphs and tables that display current levels and trends in key measures of human resource-related performance results for each category/type of employee, such as:

Employee development (scope and cost benefit)

Well-being and satisfaction

Absenteeism

Reduced safety problems

Compensation claim costs

[6.3a]

Each graph and table should contain comparative references so results can be evaluated; indicate if the comparative data are considered a world-class benchmark (best in the business), an industry standard (acceptable practice), or industry norm (average performance)
[6.3a]

6.3 Human Resource Results Item Linkages

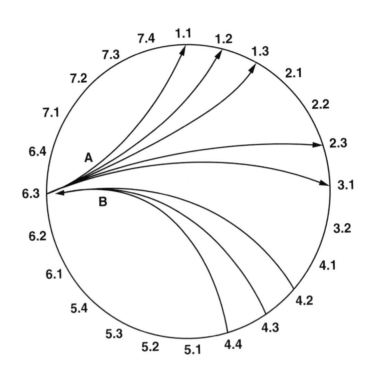

Item	Nature of Relationship
A	Human resource results data [6.3] are collected and used for planning [3.1], management decision making [1.1 or 1.2], to provide feedback to organizational managers [1.1 and 1.2] to help set human resource improvement priorities [2.3] needed. Key results in areas of public responsibility are monitored to ensure compliance with public safety and other regulatory requirements [1.3].
B	Human resource results derive from and are enhanced by improving work systems and enhancing flexibility [4.2a], and by strengthening employee recognition systems [4.2b], training [4.3], and well-being and satisfaction [4.4].

6.3 Human Resource Results—Sample Effective Practices

A. Trends and Current Levels for Supplier Performance

- The results reported in Item 6.3 derive from activities described in Item 5.3.
- Quality indices and trend data (three-year minimum preferred) are provided in graph and chart form.
- All results show steady improvement.
- Graphs and information are clear and easy to understand.
- Data are not missing.
- Comparison data for benchmark or competitor organizations are reported as appropriate.
- Trend data should be reported for employee satisfaction with working conditions, safety, retirement, and other employee benefits. Satisfaction with management should also be reported.
- Show trends for declining absenteeism, grievances, employee turnover, strikes, and worker compensation claims.

6.4 Supplier Performance Results (30 Points)

Summarize results of supplier performance and performance improvement efforts using key measures and/or indicators of such performance and improvement.

Areas to Address:

a. Current levels and trends in key measures and/or indicators of supplier performance. Graphs and tables should include appropriate comparative data.

Notes:

(1) The results reported in Item 6.4 derive from activities described in Item 5.4. Results should be broken out by key supplies and/or key suppliers, as appropriate. Results should include performance of supply chains and/or results of outsourcing, if these are important to the applicant. Data should be presented using the measures and/or indicators described in 5.4a(1).

(2) Results reported should be relative to all principal requirements: quality, delivery, and price. If the company's supplier management efforts include factors such as building supplier partnerships or reducing the number of suppliers, data related to these efforts should be included in responses.

(3) Comparative data might be of several types; industry best, best competitor(s), industry average, and appropriate benchmarks.

This item is scored using the **results** scoring guidelines. It addresses current levels and trends in key measures or indicators of supplier performance. Suppliers are external providers of materials and services "upstream" and "downstream" from the company. The focus should be on the most critical requirements from the point of view of the company—the buyer of the products and services. Data reported should reflect results by whatever means they occur—via improvements by suppliers within the supply base, through selection of better performing suppliers, or both.

Area 6.4a calls for data and current levels and trends in supplier performance. Measures and indicators of performance should relate to all key requirements—quality, delivery, and price. The area also calls for comparative information so that results reported can be evaluated against competitors or other relevant external measures of performance.

6.4 Supplier Performance Results

Results of supplier performance improvement efforts using key measures and/or indicators of such performance

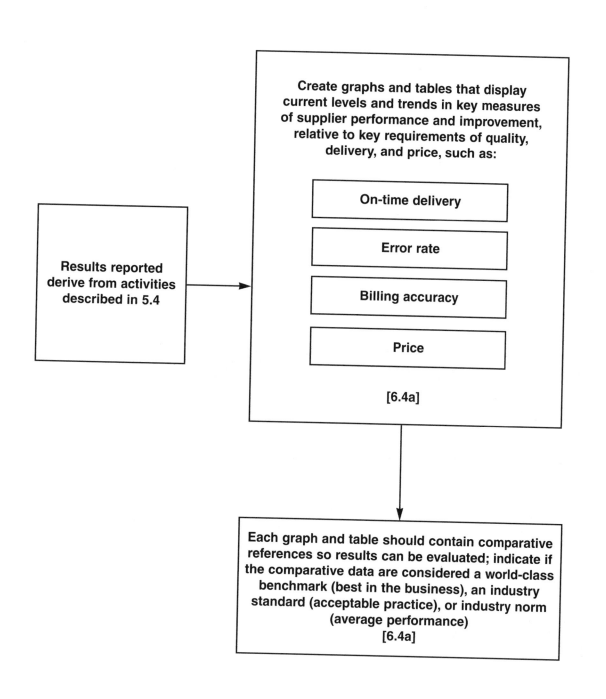

6.4 Supplier Performance Results Item Linkages

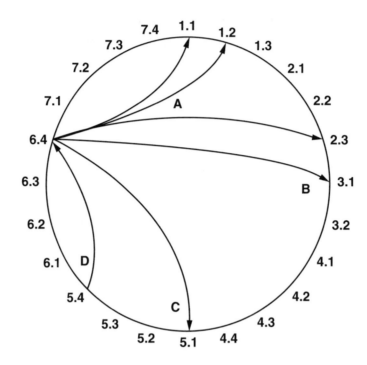

Item	Nature of Relationship
A	Supplier performance results data [6.4] are collected and used to provide feedback to suppliers and to organizational managers [1.1 and 1.2] and to help set priorities [2.3] relative to supplier performance.
B	Supplier performance results are used to determine supplier capabilities during the strategy development (planning) process [3.1].
C	Supplier capabilities are considered in the design process [5.1] to help determine overall process capability of the organization to deliver products and services to meet customer requirements.
D	Processes to improve supplier quality [5.4] affect supplier quality results [6.4].

6.4 Supplier Performance Results—Sample Effective Practices

A. Trends and Current Levels for Supplier Performance

- The results reported in Item 6.4 derive from activities described in Item 5.4.
- Results are broken out by key suppliers or supplier types as appropriate. Data are presented using the measures and indicators of supplier performance described in 5.4a, 2.1, and relevant goals in 3.2.
- If the organization's supplier management efforts include factors such as building supplier partnerships or reducing the number of suppliers, data related to these efforts are included in responses.
- Supplier performance measures include defect rate, on-time delivery, and number of certified suppliers.
- Quality indices and trend data (three-year minimum preferred) are provided in graph and chart form.
- All results show steady improvement.
- Graphs and information are clear and easy to understand.
- Data are not missing.
- Comparison data for suppliers of benchmark or competitor organizations are reported as appropriate.
- Data are broken out by meaningful supplier categories to demonstrate consistent improvement in each category.

7.0 Customer Focus and Satisfaction— 250 Points

The Customer Focus and Satisfaction category examines the company's systems for customer learning and for building and maintaining customer relationships. Also examined are levels and trends in key measures of business success—customer satisfaction and retention, market share, and satisfaction relative to competitors.

7.1 Customer and Market Knowledge (30 Points)

Describe how the company determines near-term and longer-term requirements, expectations, and preferences of customers and markets, and develops listening and learning strategies to understand and anticipate needs.

Areas to Address:

a. How the company determines current and near-term requirements and expectations of customers. Include: (1) how customer groups and/or market segments are determined and/or selected, including how customers of competitors and other potential customers are considered; (2) how information is collected, including what information is sought, frequency and methods of collection, and how objectivity and validity are ensured; (3) how specific product and service features and the relative importance of these features to customer groups or segments are determined; and (4) how other key information and data such as complaints, gains and losses of customers, and product/service performance are used to support the determination.

b. How the company addresses future requirements and expectations of customers and potential customers. Include an outline of key listening and learning strategies used.

c. How the company evaluates and improves its processes for determining customer requirements, expectations, and preferences.

Notes:

(1) The distinction between near-term and future depends upon many marketplace factors. The applicant's response should reflect these factors for its market(s). Methods used in 7.1a(2) and 7.1b might be the same or similar.

Continued on next page

(2) The company's products and services might be sold to end users via other businesses such as retail stores or dealers. Thus, "customer groups" should take into account the requirements and expectations of both the end users and these other businesses.

(3) Some companies might use similar methods to determine customer requirements/expectations and customer satisfaction (Item 7.3). In such cases, cross-references should be included.

(4) Customer groups and market segments [7.1a(1)] might take into account opportunities to select or *create* groups and segments based upon customer- and market-related information. This might include individual customization.

(5) How information is collected [7.1a(2)] might include periodic methods such as surveys or focus groups and/or ongoing processes such as dialogs with customers.

(6) Product and service features [7.1a(3)] refer to all important characteristics and to the performance of products and services that customers experience or perceive throughout their overall purchase and ownership. The focus should be primarily on features that bear upon customer preference and repurchase loyalty—for example, those features that differentiate products and services from competing offerings. This might include price and value.

(7) Examples of listening and learning strategy elements (7.1b) are:
- *relationship strategies, including close integration with customers;*
- *rapid innovation and field trials of products and services to better link R&D and design to the market;*
- *close monitoring of technological, competitive, societal, environmental, economic, and demographic factors that may bear upon customer requirements, expectations, and preferences, or alternatives;*
- *focus groups with demanding or leading-edge customers;*
- *training of frontline employees in customer listening;*
- *use of critical incidents to understand key service attributes from the point of view of customers and frontline employees;*
- *interviewing lost customers;*
- *won/lost analysis relative to competitors;*
- *post-transaction follow-up (see 7.2c); and*
- *analysis of major factors affecting key customers.*

(8) Examples of evaluation and factors appropriate for 7.1c are:
- *the adequacy and timeliness of the customer-related information;*
- *improvement of survey design;*
- *the best approaches for getting reliable and timely information—surveys, focus groups, customer-contact personnel, etc.;*
- *increasing and decreasing importance of product/service features among customer groups or segments; and*
- *the most effective listening/learning strategies.*

The evaluation might also be supported by company-level analysis addressed in Item 2.3.

This item is scored using the **approach/deployment** scoring guidelines. It addresses how the company determines current and emerging customer requirements and expectations. The thrust of the item is that many factors may affect customer preference and customer loyalty, making it necessary to listen and learn on a continual basis.

Area 7.1a calls for information on the company's process for determining current and near-term requirements and expectations of customers. Complete information regarding the customer pool is sought, including recognition of customer groups or segments and customers of competitors. Other information sought relates to sensitivity to specific product and service requirements and their relative importance to customer groups. The area is concerned with overall validity of determination methods. Validity determinations should be backed by data and information such as complaints as well as gains and losses of customers.

Area 7.1b calls for information on how the company addresses future requirements and expectations of customers—its key listening and learning strategies. Such strategies depend a great deal upon the nature of the company's products and services, the competitive environment, and relationships with customers. Listening and learning strategies should provide timely and useful information for decision making. The strategies should take into account the company's competitive strategy. For example, if the company customizes its products and services, the listening and learning strategy needs to be backed by a capable information system—one that rapidly accumulates information about customers and makes this information available where needed throughout the company.

Area 7.1c calls for information on how the company evaluates and improves its processes for determining customer requirements and expectations. Such evaluation and improvement could entail a variety of approaches—formal and informal—that enable the company to stay in close touch with customers and with issues that bear upon customer loyalty and customer preference. The purpose of the evaluation called for in Area 7.1c is to find reliable and cost-effective means to understand customer requirements and expectations on a continual basis.

7.1 Customer and Market Knowledge

How the company determines near-term and longer-term requirements and expectations of customers and markets, and develops listening and learning strategies to understand and anticipate needs

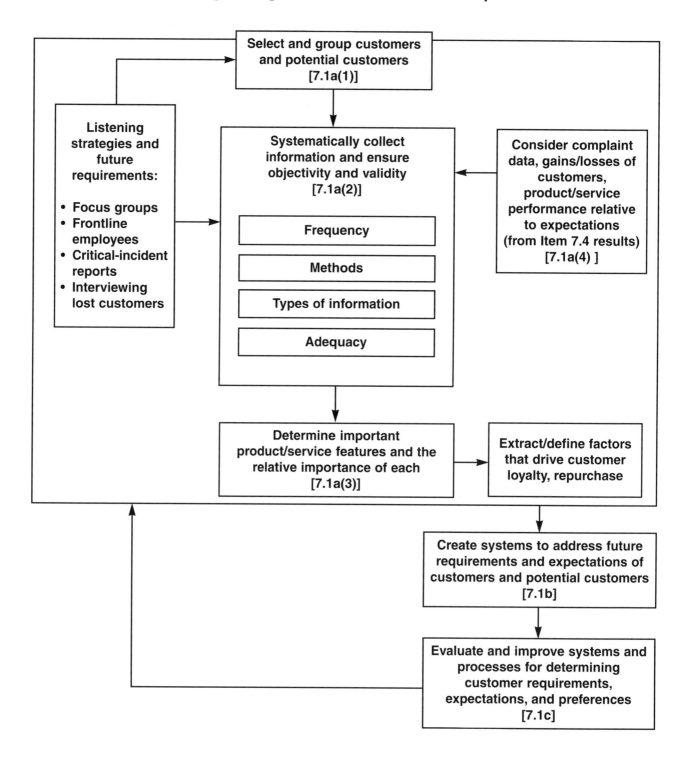

7.1 Customer and Market Knowledge Item Linkages

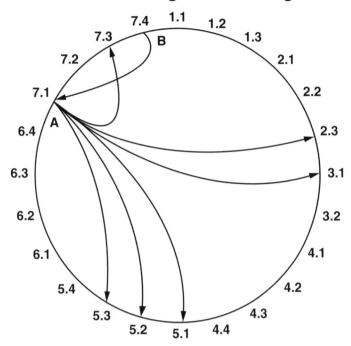

Item	Nature of Relationship
A	Information about current and future customer requirements [7.1] is used for planning [3.1], to design products and services [5.1] and revise work processes [5.2 and 5.3], to help set organizational priorities [2.3], and to build instruments to assess customer satisfaction [7.3].
B	Customer complaint data [7.4] are used to help assess current customer expectations and refine requirements [7.1].

7.1 Customer and Market Knowledge—Sample Effective Practices

A. Determining Current Customer Requirements

- Various systematic methods (for example, surveys, focus groups) are used to gather data and identify the current requirements and expectations of customers.
- Key product and service features are defined. Product and service features refer to all important characteristics and to the performance of products and services that customers experience or perceive throughout their use. The focus is primarily on factors that bear upon customer preference and loyalty—for example, those features that enhance or differentiate products and services from competing offerings.
- Customer segments are identified or grouped by customer requirements.
- Customer data such as complaints and gains or losses of customers are used to support the identification of key customer requirements.

B. Forecasting Future Customer Requirements

- Various systematic methods are used to gather data and identify the future requirements and expectations of customers.
- Customers of competitors are considered.
- Strategies for identifying key product and service features likely to be important in the future are defined. Listening and learning strategies include the following:
  - Close monitoring of technological, competitive, societal, environmental, economic, and demographic factors that may bear upon customer requirements, expectations, preferences, or alternatives
  - Focus groups with demanding or leading-edge customers
  - Training of frontline employees in customer listening
  - Use of critical incidents in product or service performance or quality to understand key service attributes from the point of view of customers and frontline employees
  - Interviewing lost customers
  - Won/lost analysis relative to competitors
  - Analysis of major factors affecting key customers

C. *Improving Customer Requirements Definition and Forecasting Processes*

- Data gathering and forecasting methods are evaluated and improved through several cycles. Examples of factors that are evaluated include the following:
    - The adequacy and timeliness of the customer-related information, improvement of survey design
    - Approaches for getting reliable and timely information—surveys, focus groups, customer-contact personnel
    - Effective listening/learning strategies
- Best practices for gathering customer requirements and forecasting are gathered and used to make improvements.

7.2 Customer Relationship Management (30 Points)

Describe how the company provides effective management of its responses and follow-ups with customers to preserve and build relationships, to increase knowledge about specific customers and about general customer expectations, to improve company performance, and to generate ideas for new products and services.

Areas to Address:

a. How the company provides information and easy access to enable customers to seek information and assistance, to comment, and to complain. Describe how contact management performance is measured. Include key service standards and how these standards are set, deployed, and tracked.

b. How the company ensures that formal and informal complaints and feedback received by all company units are resolved effectively and promptly. Briefly describe the complaint management process, including how it ensures effective recovery of customer confidence, how it meets customer requirements for resolution effectiveness, how it ensures that complaints received by company units are aggregated and analyzed for use throughout the company, and how it seeks to eliminate causes of complaints.

c. How the company follows up with customers on products, services, and recent transactions to determine satisfaction, to resolve problems, to seek feedback for improvement, to build relationships, and to develop ideas for new products and services.

d. How the company evaluates and improves its customer relationship management. Include: (1) how service standards, including those related to access and complaint management, are improved based upon customer information; and (2) how knowledge about customers is accumulated.

Notes:

(1) Customer relationship management refers to a process, not to a company unit. However, some companies might have units which address all or most of the requirements included in this Item. Also, some of these requirements might be included among the responsibilities of frontline employees in processes described in Items 5.2 and 5.3.

(2) How the company maintains easy access for customers (7.2a) might involve close integration, electronic networks, etc.

(3) Performance measures and service standards (7.2a) apply not only to employees providing the responses to customers, but also to other units within the company that

Continued on next page

make effective responses possible. Deployment needs to take into account all key points in a response chain. Examples of measures and standards are: telephonic, percentage of resolutions achieved by frontline employees, number of transfers, and resolution response time.

(4) Responses to 7.2b and 7.2c might include company processes for addressing customer complaints or comments based upon expressed or implied guarantees and warranties.

(5) The complaint management process (7.2b) might include analysis and priority setting for improvement projects based upon potential cost impact of complaints, taking into account customer retention related to resolution effectiveness. Some of the analysis requirements of Item 7.2 relate to Item 2.3.

(6) Improvement of customer relationship management (7.2d) might require training. Training for customer-contact (frontline) employees should address: (a) key knowledge and skills, including knowledge of products and services; (b) listening to customers; (c) soliciting comments from customers; (d) how to anticipate and handle problems or failures ("recovery"); (e) skills in customer retention; and (f) how to manage expectations. Such training should be described in Item 4.3.

(7) Information on trends and levels in measures and/or indicators of complaint response time, effective resolution, and percent of complaints resolved on first contact should be reported in Item 6.1.

Item 7.2 is scored using the **approach/deployment** scoring guidelines. It addresses how the company effectively manages its responses and follow-ups with customers. Relationship management provides a potentially important means for companies to understand and manage customer expectations. Also, front-line employees may provide vital information useful in building part-nerships and other longer-term relationships with customers.

Area 7.2a calls for information on how the company provides easy access for customers specifically for purposes of seeking information or assistance and to comment and complain. This area also calls for information on service standards and their use. Service standards are measures of performance with expectations of service performance defined. For example, quick response to customer complaints is a goal. The measure is time between complaint and response. The standard defines a specific time expectation, such as "respond within two hours."

Area 7.2b focuses on the complaint management process. The principal issue addressed is prompt and effective resolution of complaints, including recovery of customer confidence. The area also addresses how the company learns from complaints and ensures that production and delivery process employees (Items 5.1, 5.2, 5.3, and sometimes 5.4) receive information needed to eliminate the causes of complaints.

Area 7.2c calls for information on how the company follows up with customers regarding products, services, and recent transactions to determine satisfaction, to resolve problems, and to gather information for improvement or for new services. This information is quickly made available to production and delivery process employees.

Area 7.2d calls for information on how the company evaluates and improves its customer response management. Improvements may be of several types. Examples include improving service standards, such as complaint resolution time and resolution effectiveness, and improving the use of customer feedback to improve production and delivery processes, training, and hiring.

7.2 Customer Relationship Management

How the company provides effective management of its responses and follow-ups with customers to preserve and build relationships and to increase knowledge about specific customers and about general customer expectations

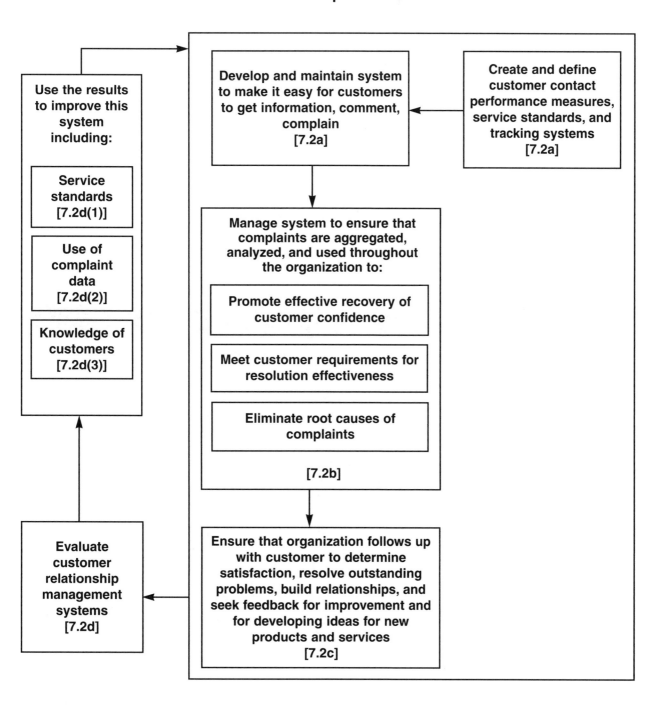

7.2 Customer Relationship Management Item Linkages

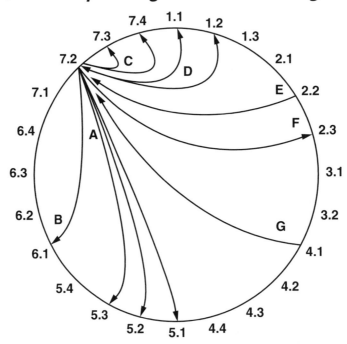

Item	Nature of Relationship
A	Information collected through customer relations employees [7.2] is used to enhance design of products and services [5.1] and improve operational and support processes [5.2 and 5.3].
B	Efforts of customer relations systems should result in improved complaint response time, effective complaint resolution, and percent of complaints resolved on first contact. These results should be reported in 6.1.
C	Information from customer relations processes can help in the design of customer satisfaction measures [7.3] and even produce data on customer satisfaction [7.4].
D	Priorities and service standards of customer service personnel [7.2] are driven by top leadership [1.1]. Managers at all levels [1.1 and 1.2] personally interact with and build better relationships with customers. They receive useful information from those customers to improve management decision making.
E	Benchmark data [2.2] are used to set service standards [7.2].
F	Customer relations data are analyzed and used to set priorities for action [2.3].
G	Human resource development plans [4.1] address the development and empowerment of frontline, customer-contact employees.

7.2 Customer Relationship Management—Sample Effective Practices

A. Easy Access for Customers

- Several methods are used to ensure ease of customer contact 24 hours daily, if necessary (for example, toll-free numbers, pagers for contact personnel, surveys, interviews, focus groups, electronic bulletin boards).
- Requirements for building relationships are identified and may include factors such as product knowledge, employee responsiveness, and various customer contact methods.
- Customer contact employees are empowered to make decisions to address customer concerns.
- Adequate staff are available to maintain effective customer contact.
- Performance expectations are set for employees whose job brings them in regular contact with customers.
- The performance of employees against these expectations is measured and tracked.

B. Complaint Management

- A system exists to ensure that customer complaints are resolved promptly and effectively.
- Complaints and customer concerns are resolved at first contact. This often means training customer contact employees and giving them authority for resolving a broad range of problems.
- Complaint data are tracked and used to initiate prompt corrective action to prevent the problem from recurring.
- Problem resolution priority setting is based on the potential cost impact of customer decisions to repurchase or recommend the product or service to others.

C. Customer Follow-Up

- Procedures are in place and evaluated to ensure that customer contact is initiated to follow up on recent transactions to build relationships.
- Feedback is sought on the effectiveness of service.

D. Improving Customer Relationship Management

- A systematic approach to evaluate and improve service and customer relationships exists.
- Feedback from customers and employees is used in the improvement process.
- Training and development plans and replacement procedures for customer contact employees exist.
- Objective customer service standards have been derived from customer expectations (for example, timeliness, courtesy, efficiency, thoroughness, and completeness).

7.3 Customer Satisfaction Determination (30 Points)

Describe how the company determines customer satisfaction, customer repurchase intentions, and customer satisfaction relative to competitors; describe how these determination processes are evaluated and improved.

Areas to Address:

a. How the company determines customer satisfaction. Include: (1) a brief description of processes and measurement scales used; frequency of determination; and how objectivity and validity are ensured. Indicate significant differences, if any, in processes and measurement scales for different customer groups or segments; and (2) how customer satisfaction measurements capture key information that reflects customers' likely future market behavior.

b. How customer satisfaction relative to that of competitors is determined. Describe: (1) company-based comparative studies; and (2) comparative studies or evaluations made by independent organizations and/or customers. For (1) and (2), describe how objectivity and validity of studies or evaluations are ensured.

c. How the company evaluates and improves its overall processes and measurement scales for determining customer satisfaction and satisfaction relative to competitors. Include how other indicators (such as gains and losses of customers) and dissatisfaction indicators (such as complaints) are used in this improvement process. Describe also how the evaluation determines the effectiveness of companywide use of customer satisfaction information and data.

Notes:

(1) Customer satisfaction measurement might include both a numerical rating scale and descriptors for each unit in the scale. An effective (actionable) customer satisfaction measurement system provides reliable information about customer ratings of specific product and service features and the relationship between these ratings and the customer's likely future market behavior—repurchase and/or positive referral. Product and service features might include overall value and price.

(2) The company's products and services might be sold to end users via other businesses such as retail stores or dealers. Thus, "customer groups" or segments should take into account these other businesses and the end users.

(3) Customer dissatisfaction indicators include complaints, claims, refunds, recalls, returns, repeat services, litigation, replacements, downgrades, repairs, warranty work, warranty costs, misshipments, and incomplete orders.

Continued on next page

(4) Comparative studies (7.3b) might include indicators of customer dissatisfaction as well as satisfaction.

(5) Evaluation (7.3c) might take into account:
- *how well the measurement scale relates to actual customer behavior;*
- *the effectiveness of pre-survey research used in survey design;*
- *how well customer responses link to key business processes and thus provide actionable information for improvement; and*
- *how well customer responses have been translated into cost/revenue implications and thus provide actionable information for improvement priorities.*

(6) Use of data from satisfaction measurement is called for in 5.2b(4) and 5.3c(4). Such data also provide key input to analysis [Item 2.3].

This item is scored using the **approach/deployment** scoring guidelines. It addresses how the company determines customer satisfaction and satisfaction relative to competitors.

Area 7.3a calls for information on how the company gathers information on customer satisfaction, including any important differences in approaches for different customer groups or segments. The area highlights the importance of the measurement scale to focus on the factors that reflect customers' market behaviors—repurchase, new business, and positive referral.

Area 7.3b calls for information on how satisfaction relative to competitors is determined. Such information might be derived from company-based comparative studies or studies made by independent organizations. The purpose of this comparison is to develop information that can be used for improving performance relative to competitors and to better understand the factors that drive markets.

Area 7.3c calls for information on how the company evaluates and improves its processes and measurement scales for determining customer satisfaction and satisfaction relative to competitors. This evaluation and improvement process is expected to draw upon other indicators such as gains and losses of customers and customer dissatisfaction indicators such as complaints. The evaluation should also consider how well customer satisfaction information and data are used throughout the company. Such use is likely to be enhanced if data are presented in an actionable form meeting two key conditions: (1) survey responses tying directly to key business processes; and (2) survey responses translated into cost and revenue implications.

7.3 Customer Satisfaction Determination

**How the company determines customer satisfaction
and customer repurchase intentions**

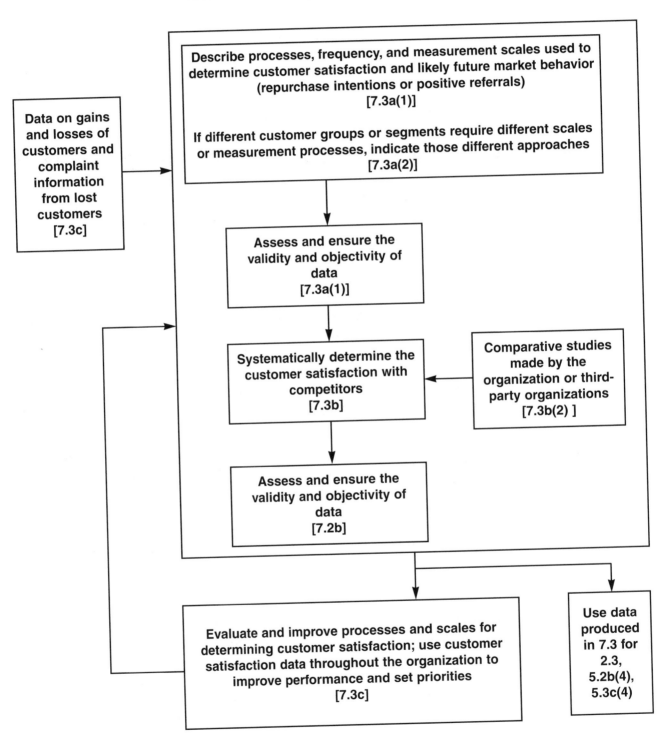

Data on gains and losses of customers and complaint information from lost customers [7.3c]

Describe processes, frequency, and measurement scales used to determine customer satisfaction and likely future market behavior (repurchase intentions or positive referrals) [7.3a(1)]

If different customer groups or segments require different scales or measurement processes, indicate those different approaches [7.3a(2)]

Assess and ensure the validity and objectivity of data [7.3a(1)]

Systematically determine the customer satisfaction with competitors [7.3b]

Comparative studies made by the organization or third-party organizations [7.3b(2)]

Assess and ensure the validity and objectivity of data [7.2b]

Evaluate and improve processes and scales for determining customer satisfaction; use customer satisfaction data throughout the organization to improve performance and set priorities [7.3c]

Use data produced in 7.3 for 2.3, 5.2b(4), 5.3c(4)

7.3 Customer Satisfaction Determination Item Linkages

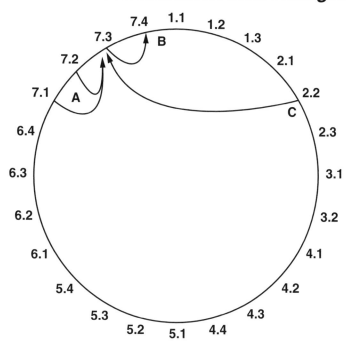

Item	Nature of Relationship
A	Information about current and future customer requirements [7.1] and data collected through customer contact [7.2] are used to build instruments to assess customer satisfaction [7.3].
B	Processes used to determine customer satisfaction [7.3] produce data on levels of satisfaction and the satisfaction levels enjoyed by competitors or comparison organizations [7.4].
C	Benchmark data [2.2] are used to design instruments and processes to assess customer satisfaction [7.3].

7.3 Customer Satisfaction Determination—Sample Effective Practices

A. Determining Customer Satisfaction

- An actionable customer satisfaction measurement system exists that provides the organization with reliable information about customer ratings of specific product and service features and the relationship between these ratings and the customer's likely future market behavior (loyalty).
- Several customer satisfaction indicators are used (for example, repeat business, praise letters, and direct measures using survey questions and interviews).
- Comprehensive satisfaction and dissatisfaction data are collected and segmented or grouped to enable the organization to predict customer behavior (likelihood of remaining a customer).
- Several means of collecting customer satisfaction data are used (for example, surveys, interviews, or third-party contractors).
- Customer satisfaction measurement includes both a numerical rating scale and descriptors assigned to each unit in the scale. An effective (actionable) customer satisfaction measurement system provides the organization with reliable information about customer ratings of specific product and service features and the relationship between these ratings and the customer's likely market behavior.
- Customer dissatisfaction indicators include complaints, claims, refunds, recalls, returns, repeat services, litigation, replacements, performance rating downgrades, repairs, warranty work, warranty costs, misshipments, and incomplete orders.
- Satisfaction data are collected from lost customers

B. Comparison with Competitors

- Competitors' customer satisfaction is determined using various means such as external or internal studies.
- Methods are in place to ensure objectivity of these data.
- Organization-based or independent organization comparative studies take into account one or more indicators of customer dissatisfaction as well as satisfaction. The extent and types of such studies depend upon industry and organization size.

C. Improving the Process of Determining Customer Satisfaction

- The process of collecting complete, timely, and accurate customer satisfaction and dissatisfaction data is regularly evaluated and improved.
- Several improvement cycles are evident.

7.4 Customer Satisfaction Results (160 Points)

Summarize the company's customer satisfaction and customer dissatisfaction results using key measures and/or indicators or these results. Compare results with competitors' results.

Areas to Address:

a. Current levels and trends in key measures and/or indicators of customer satisfaction and dissatisfaction. Results should be segmented by customer groups and product and service types, as appropriate.

b. Current levels and trends in key measures and/or indicators of customer satisfaction relative to competitors. Results should be segmented by customer groups and product and service types, as appropriate.

Notes:

(1) Results reported in this Item derive from methods described in Items 7.3 and 7.2.

(2) Measures and/or indicators of satisfaction relative to competitors (7.4b) should include gains and losses of customers and customer accounts to competitors as well as gains and losses in market share.

(3) Measures and/or indicators of satisfaction relative to competitors might include objective information and/or data from independent organizations, including customers. Examples include survey results, competitive awards, recognition, and ratings. Such information and data should reflect comparative satisfaction (and dissatisfaction), not comparative performance or products and services (called for in Item 6.1).

(4) Customer retention data might be used in both 7.4a and 7.4b. For example, in 7.4a, customer retention might be included as a satisfaction indicator, while in 7.4b, customer retention relative to competitors might be part of a switching analysis to determine competitive position and the factors responsible for it.

This item is scored using the **results** scoring guidelines. It addresses two related but nevertheless different types of business results—customer satisfaction and customer dissatisfaction.

Area 7.4a calls for information on trends and current levels in key measures or indicators of customer satisfaction and dissatisfaction. The presentation of results could include information on customer retention and other appropriate evidence of current and recent past satisfaction with the company's products and services, such as customer awards.

Measures or indicators of dissatisfaction depend upon the nature of the products or services. Item 7.3, Note (3), lists a number of possible indicators of dissatisfaction. In addition, a company's survey methods might include a scale that uses ratings such as "very dissatisfied" or "somewhat dissatisfied."

The reason for including measures of both satisfaction and dissatisfaction is that they usually provide different information. The factors in high levels of satisfaction may not be the same factors as those that produce high levels of dissatisfaction. In addition, the effect of individual instances of dissatisfaction on overall satisfaction could vary widely depending upon the effectiveness of the company's resolution ("recovery") of a problem.

Item 7.4 provide a complete picture of customer satisfaction. In the chart below, customer satisfaction is improving. However, if market share is declining—that is, the organization is losing customers—it may not be as totally healthy as originally thought.

Although Item 7.4 is a results item, it is anticipated that the results themselves are input drivers of improvement priorities—actions that affect customer retention and positive referral. That is, the main management approach involves viewing increasing satisfaction and decreasing dissatisfaction as a means, not an end. The end is retention and positive referral. Use of customer satisfaction data and information is called for in Item 2.3.

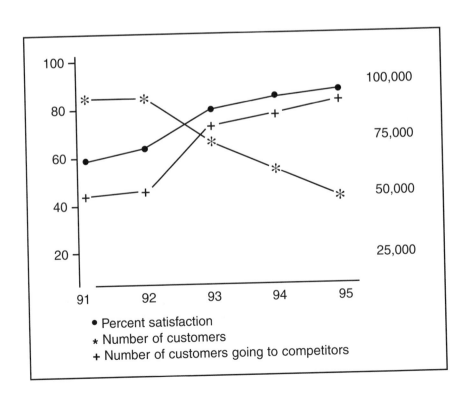

7.4 Customer Satisfaction Results

The company's customer satisfaction and customer dissatisfaction results using key measures and/or indicators of these results

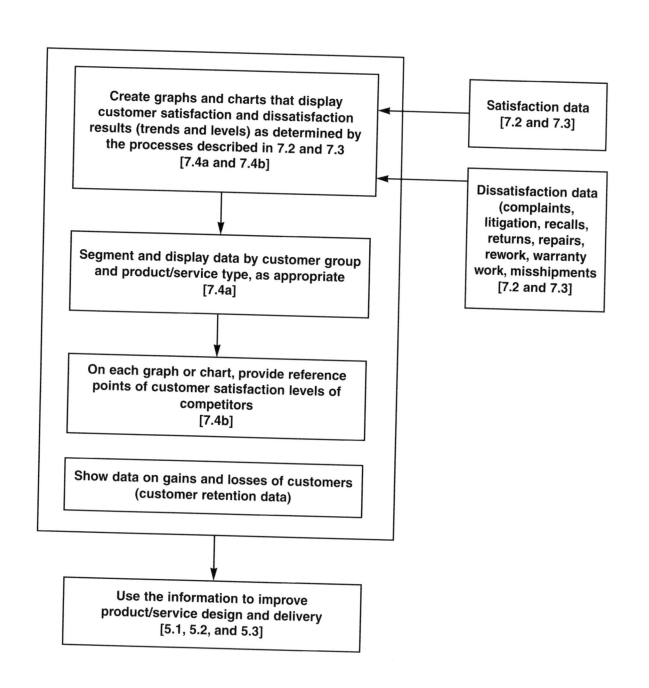

7.4 *Customer Satisfaction Results Item Linkages*

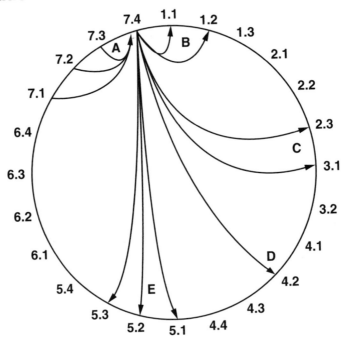

Item	Nature of Relationship
A	Processes used to gather intelligence about current customer requirements [7.1], strengthen customer relations [7.2], and determine customer satisfaction [7.3] produce customer satisfaction data [7.4].
B	Data on levels of satisfaction of customers [7.4] are monitored by executives [1.1] and managers at all levels [1.2].
C	Data on levels of satisfaction of customers [7.4] are collected [2.1] and used to set organizational priorities, allocate resources [2.3], and for strategic planning [3.1].
D	Recognition and rewards [4.2b] are based, in part, on customer satisfaction results [7.4].
E	Data on satisfaction of customers [7.4] are used to help design products and services [5.1], and improve operational [5.2] and support [5.3] processes.

7.4 Customer Satisfaction Results—Sample Effective Practices

A. Customer Satisfaction

- Trends (three-year minimum preferred) and indicators of customer satisfaction, segmented by customer groups, are provided in graph and chart form for all key measures.
- All indicators show steady improvement. (Indicators include data collected in 7.3 such as customer assessments of products and services, customer awards, and customer retention.)
- Customer satisfaction graphs and information are accurate and easy to understand.
- Data are not missing.
- Results data are supported by customer feedback, customers' overall assessments of products and services, and customer awards.

B. Customer Dissatisfaction

- Data are presented concerning customer dissatisfaction for the most relevant product or service quality indicators collected through the processes described in 7.3 (some of which may be referenced in the key business factors in the overview).

Tips on Preparing a Baldrige Award Application

Organizational Self-Assessment

Team Membership

The process for preparing a Baldrige Award application starts with a thorough self-assessment of your organization using the Baldrige Award criteria. We recommend forming a team of employees and managers to do the analysis. Team members, collectively, should broadly understand the entire organization and its major systems, processes, and customers. They should also understand the Baldrige Award criteria and scoring system. Individual team members may have special expertise in one or more categories of the award criteria. If the team has not done a Baldrige Award or similar assessment, a short one- to two-day training course will significantly improve team effectiveness and the assessment quality.

Team membership should vary according to organization size and complexity. Smaller teams (four to eight members) are easier to manage and help ensure that the analysis and report are cohesive. Larger teams (14 to 21 members) distribute the workload, which can be extensive, but require more coordination and increase the risks of producing a disjointed application.

A seven-member team is the recommended minimum. Under this configuration each team member "owns" the initial analysis for a category and serves as back-up for another. With larger teams, two to three people work each category and each owns one or more Items in that category.

Team Operations

Team leadership may be shared, rotated, or assigned to a member (who also owns a category or item). Effective meeting management techniques should be practiced. Create and follow an agenda. Use a timekeeper. Record team discussions and decisions on a flip chart. From the real-time records, prepare team minutes. Rotate record keeping (scribe) responsibilities. Evaluate and improve meeting effectiveness—even your process for assessing your management systems should role-model continuous improvement.

Scoring Guidelines

You have already carefully examined the Baldrige Award Criteria. Now study what is required by the scoring guidelines (which appear on the next page). Together, the criteria and scoring guidelines form a diagnostic system. Depending on the requirements of the item, scoring is based on the approach and deployment of the process required or on the results of the processes.

Official Scoring Guidelines

	Approach and Deployment
0%	• No systematic approach evident
10% to 30%	• Beginning of a systematic approach to the primary purposes of the item • Early stages of a transition from reacting to problems to a general improvement orientation • Major gaps exist in deployment that would inhibit progress in achieving the primary purposes of the item
40% to 60%	• A sound, systematic approach, responsive to the primary purposes of the item • A fact-based improvement process in place in key areas; more emphasis is placed on improvement than on reaction to problems • No major gaps in deployment, though some areas of work units may be in very early stages of deployment
70% to 90%	• A sound, systematic approach, responsive to the overall purposes of the item • A fact-based improvement process is a key management tool; clear evidence of refinement and improved integration as a result of improvement cycles and analysis • Approach is well-deployed, with no major gaps; deployment may vary in some areas or work units
100%	• A sound, systematic approach, fully responsive to all the requirements of the item • A very strong, fact-based improvement process is a key management tool; strong refinement and integration—backed by excellent analysis • Approach is fully deployed without any significant weaknesses or gaps in any areas or work units
	Results
0%	• No results, or poor results in areas reported
10% to 30%	• Early stages of developing trends; some improvement and/or early good performance levels in a few areas • Results not reported for many to most areas of importance to the applicant's key business requirements
40% to 60%	• Improvement trends and/or good performance levels reported for many to most areas of importance to the applicant's key business requirements • No pattern of adverse trends and/or poor performance levels in areas of importance to the applicant's key business requirements • Some trends and/or current performance levels—evaluated against relevant comparisons and/or benchmarks—show areas of strength and/or good to very good relative performance levels
70% to 90%	• Current performance is good to excellent in most areas of importance to the applicant's key business requirements • Most improvement trends and/or performance levels are sustained • Many to most trends and/or current performance levels—evaluated against relevant comparisons and/or benchmarks—show areas of leadership and very good relative performance levels
100%	• Current performance is excellent in most areas of importance to the applicant's key business requirements • Excellent improvement trends and/or sustained excellent performance levels in most areas • Strong evidence of industry and benchmark leadership demonstrated in many areas

Supplementary Scoring Guidelines

Approach/ Deployment

1. For approach/deployment items, first determine the appropriate level on the approach scale.

2. Then read the corresponding level on the deployment scale. For example, if the approach level is 40 percent, read the 40 percent standard on the deployment scale where one would expect "a few major gaps in deployment exist and many work units are in the early stages of development." If that is the case, the final score is 40 percent.

3. However, if the deployment score is low, reduce the final score somewhat. For example, if only "isolated units are using quality practices; most are not," you

would reduce the 40 percent approach score to a 20 percent to 30 percent final score.

4. *Never increase the approach score based on deployment.*

Results

1. For results items, base your assessment only on the standards described on the results scale. *Do not consider approach or deployment standards at all.*

2. Determine the extent to which performance results are positive, complete, and at high levels relative to competitors or an industry standard.

3. To determine the extent to which all important results are reported, examiners should develop a list of the key measures the applicant indicates are important. Start with the measures listed in the overview section. Then add to the key measures from data reported in item 2.1 and the goals in 3.2. Key measures can be reported anywhere in an application.

Score	Approach	Deployment	Results
0%	Anecdotal, no systematic approach evident.	Anecdotal, undocumented.	No results or poor results in areas reported.
10%	Beginning of a systematic approach consistent with the overall purposes of the item. Generally reactive approach to problems.	Isolated units are using quality practices most are not.	Data not reported for most areas of importance to the applicant's key business requirements. Limited positive results and trends.
20%	A systematic approach consistent with the overall purposes of the item is evident to a limited extent. Still reactive to problems.	Some units are using quality practices; most are not.	Data not reported for many to most areas of importance to the applicant's key business requirements. Some positive results and trends.
30%	A systematic approach responsive to the overall purposes of the item is evolving. Transitioning from reactive to proactive problem solving (prevention).	Some major gaps in deployment still exist (requirements of the item not addressed or not practiced by major components.	Data not reported for many areas of importance to the applicant's key business requirements. Several positive results and quantifiable improvement trends reported.
40%	Systematic approach, responsive to the overall purposes of the item. Emphasis on prevention but no evaluation or improvement system is in place. Some fact-based decision processes are evident.	A few major gaps in deployment exist. Many work units in the early stages of deployment.	Data are reported for most key areas of importance to the applicant's key business requirements. Generally positive trends reported for many areas of importance to the applicant's key business requirements.
50%	Prevention and fact-based quality system is responsive to the overall purposes of the item and includes process evaluation (but no refinements are in place).	No major gaps in deployment exist. Some work units may still be in the early stages of development.	Data are reported for most key areas of importance to the applicant's business requirements with positive trends in most key areas important to the item and key business factors. Some trends can be evaluated against benchmarks or comparisons.
60%	Prevention and fact-based quality system is responsive to the overall purposes of the item with at least one evaluation and improvement cycle completed, including some refinement.	No major gaps in deployment exist. A few work units may still be in the early stages of development.	Data are reported for most key areas of importance to the applicant's business requirements with no significant adverse trends. Good performance in most key areas important to the item and key business factors. Several trends can be evaluated against benchmarks or comparisons.
70%	Prevention, fact-based, integrated quality system is responsive to the overall purposes of the item. Several evaluation and improvement cycles and refinements.	No major gaps in deployment with most work units in the middle to advanced stages of development.	Good improvement trends reported with no adverse trends in all key areas important to the item and key business factors. Many trends can be evaluated against benchmarks or comparisons.
90%	Prevention, fact-based, integrated quality systems are responsive to the overall purposes of the item. Several evaluation and improvement cycles and substantial innovative refinements.	No major gaps in deployment with most work units in the advanced stages of development.	Excellent results and sustained positive trends (no adverse trends) in all key areas important to the item and key business factors. Most trends can be evaluated against benchmarks or comparisons.
100%	Prevention and fact-based quality systems are fully responsive to all of the purposes of the item with continuous evaluation and improvement cycles and substantial innovative refinements.	Approach is fully deployed to all work units with no gaps in deployment. All work units in the advanced stages of deployment.	Excellent (world-class) results and strong sustained trends in all areas important to the item and key business factors. Strong evidence of benchmark leadership.

Approach/Deployment

Systemic　　Look for evidence of a system—a repeatable, predictable process that is used to fulfill the requirements of the item. Briefly describe the system. Be sure to explain *how* the system works. You must communicate the nature of the system to people who are not familiar with it. This is essential to achieve the 30 percent scoring threshold.

Integrated　　Determine the extent to which the system integrated or linked with other elements of the overall management system. Show the linkages across categories for key themes such as those displayed for each item earlier in this book.

Consider the extent to which the work of senior leadership is integrated. For example,

1. Senior executives [Item 1.1] are responsible for shaping and communicating the organization's vision, values, and expectations throughout the leadership system and workforce.

2. They develop relationships with key customers [Item 7.2] and monitor customer satisfaction [Item 7.4] and organization performance [Items 6.1, 6.2, 6.3, 6.4].

3. This information, when properly analyzed [2.3], helps them set priorities and allocate resources to optimize customer satisfaction and operational and financial performance.

4. With this in mind, senior executives participate in strategy development [Item 3.1] and ensure the alignment of the workplace to achieve organizational goals [Item 3.2].

5. Senior executives may also become involved in supporting new structures to improve employee performance [Item 4.2], training effectiveness [Item 4.3], and employee well-being and satisfaction [Item 4.4].

Similar relationships (linkages) exist between other Items. Highlight these linkages to demonstrate integration.

Prevention-Based　Prevention-based systems are characterized by actions to minimize or prevent the recurrence of problems. In an ideal world, all systems would produce perfect products and flawless service. Since that rarely happens, high performing organizations are able to act quickly to recover from a problem (fight the fire) and then take action to identify the root cause of the problem and prevent it from surfacing again. The nature of the problem, its root cause, and appropriate corrective action are communicated to all relevant employees so they can implement the correction action in their area before the problem arises.

Continuous Improvement

Continuous improvement is a bedrock theme. It is the method that helps organizations keep their competitive edge. Continuous improvement involves evaluation and improvement of processes crucial to organizational success. Evaluation and improvement completes the high performance management cycle. Continuous improvement evaluations can be complex, data-driven, statistical processes or as simple as a focus group discussing "What went right, what went wrong, and how can it be done better?" The key to optimum performance lies in the pervasive evaluation and improvement of all processes. By practicing systematic, pervasive, continuous improvement, time becomes the organization's ally. Consistent evaluation and refinement practices can drive the score to 60 percent or 70 percent, and higher.

Complete

Each item contains one or more areas to address. Many areas to address contain several parts. Failure to address all areas and parts can push the score lower. If an area to address or part of an area does not apply to your organization, it is important to explain why. Otherwise, examiners may conclude the system is incomplete.

Innovative

The highest scoring organization is able to demonstrate that its process is innovative, unique, world class, and a trendsetter. When the process is so good that it becomes the benchmark for others (and is deployed throughout the organization), the score moves to the 90 percent to 100 percent range.

Anecdotal

If your assessment describes a process that is essentially anecdotal and does not systematically address the criteria, it is worth very little (0 to 10 points).

Deployment

The extent to which processes are widely used by organization units affects scoring. For example, a systematic approach that is well integrated, evaluated consistently, and refined routinely may be worth 70 percent to 90 percent. However, if that process is not in place in all key parts of the organization, the 70 percent to 90 percent score will be reduced, perhaps significantly, depending on the nature and extent of the gap.

Major gaps are expected to exist at the 0 percent to 30 percent level. At the 40 percent to 60 percent level, no major gaps exist, although some units may still be at the early stages of development. At the 70 percent to 90 percent level, no major gaps exist and many to most units are in the advanced stages of development in the area called for in the criteria.

Summary

For each item examined, the process is rated as follows:

- Anecdotal: 0 percent to 10 percent
- Systematic: 10 percent to 30 percent
- Fully developed: 40 percent
- Prevention-based and evaluated: 50 percent
- Refined: 60 percent to 80 percent
- Widely used with no gaps in deployment: 70+ percent

Systematic, integrated, prevention-based, and continuously improved systems that are widely used are generally easier to describe than undeveloped systems. Moreover, describing numerous activities or anecdotes does not convince examiners that an integrated, prevention-based system is in place. In fact, simply describing numerous activities and anecdotes suggests that a system does not exist. However, by tracing critical success threads through the relevant items in the criteria, the organization demonstrates that its system is integrated and more fully deployed.

To demonstrate system integration, pick several critical success factors and show how the organization manages them. For example, trace the leadership focus on performance.
- Identify performance-related data that are collected to indicate progress against goals [Item 2.1].
- Show how leaders analyze performance data to set work priorities [Item 2.3].
- Show how performance effectiveness is considered in the planning process and how work at all levels is aligned to increase performance.
- Demonstrate the impact of human resource management [Item 4.2] and training [Item 4.3] on performance.
- Show how design, development, production, and delivery processes [Items 5.1, 5.2, 5.3] are enhanced to improve results.
- Report the results of improved performance [6.1, 6.2, 6.3, and 6.4].
- Determine how improved performance affects customer satisfaction levels [Item 7.4].
- Show how customer concerns are used to drive the selection of key measures.

Note that the application is limited to 70 pages, not including the four-page Business Overview. This may not be sufficient to describe in great detail the approach, deployment, results, and systematic integration of all of your critical success factors, goals, or key processes. Thus, you must pick the most important few, indicating them as such, then thoroughly describe the threads and linkages throughout the application.

Guidelines for Responding to Approach/Deployment Items

Approach/deployment items permit diagnosis of the applicant's most important systems, activities, and processes—the ones that offer the greatest potential for fast-paced improvement of the applicant's performance. Diagnosis and feedback depend heavily upon the content and completeness of approach/deployment item responses. For this reason, it is important to respond to these items by providing key process information. Guidelines for organizing such information are given below.

Understand the Meaning of How

Items that request information on approach include areas to address that begin with the word *how*. Responses to such areas should provide a complete picture to enable meaningful evaluation and feedback. Responses should outline key process details such as methods, measures, deployment, and evaluation factors. Information lacking sufficient detail to permit an evaluation and feedback, or merely providing an example, is referred to in the criteria booklet as anecdotal information.

Show What and How

Describe your system for meeting the requirements of each item. Ensure that methods, processes, and practices are fully described. Use flowcharts to help examiners visualize your key processes.

It is important to give basic information about what key processes are and how they work. Although it is helpful to include who performs the work, merely stating who does not permit feedback. For example, stating that "customer satisfaction data are analyzed for improvement by the Customer Service Department" does not set the stage for useful feedback because, from this very limited information, potential strengths and weaknesses in the analysis cannot be identified at all.

Show That Activities Are Systematic

Ensure that the response describes a systematic approach, not merely an anecdotal example.

Approaches that are systematic use data and information for cycles of improvement. In other words, the approaches are systematic over time and thus show learning and maturity. Scores above 50 percent rely upon clear evidence that approaches are systematic.

Show Deployment	Ensure that the response gives clear and sufficient information on deployment. For example, from a response, one must be able to distinguish whether an approach described is used in one, some, most, or all parts of the organization. Deployment can be shown compactly by using summary tables that outline what is done in different parts of the organization. This is particularly effective if the basic approach is described in a narrative.
Show Focus, Consistency, and Integration	The response demonstrates that your organization is focused on key processes and on improvements that offer the greatest potential to improve business performance. There are four important factors to consider regarding setting the stage for consistency and integration: (1) the Business Overview should make clear what is important; (2) the Strategic Planning Category, including the key business drivers (key result areas), should highlight areas of greatest focus and describe how deployment is accomplished; (3) descriptions of organization-level analysis (Item 2.3) should show how the organization analyzes performance information to set priorities; and (4) organization-level review (1.2b) should show how performance information is tracked and used. Focus, consistency, and integration in the approach/deployment items should be accompanied by corresponding results being reported in Items 6.1, 6.2, 6.3, 6.4, and 7.4.
Respond Fully to Item Requirements	Ensure that the response fully addresses all important parts of each item and each area to address. Missing information will be interpreted as a gap in approach and/or deployment. All areas should be addressed and checked in final review.
Cross-Reference When Appropriate	Applicants should try to make each item response self-contained. However, there may be instances when responses to different items are mutually reinforcing. It is then appropriate to reference responses to other items, rather than to repeat information. In such cases, applicants should use area designators (for example, "see 2.3a").

Guidelines for Responding to Results Items

The award criteria place greatest emphasis on results. Items 6.1, 6.2, 6.3, 6.4, and 7.4 call for results related to all key requirements, stakeholders, and goals.

Five key requirements for effective presentation of results data include:

- Trends show directions of results and rates of change.

- Performance levels show performance on some meaningful measurement scale.

- Comparisons show how trends and/or levels compare with those of other, appropriately selected organizations.

- Breadth of results shows completeness of deployment of improvement activities.

- Focus shows that results reported are consistent with and cover the most important requirements for business success, highlighted in the business overview and included in responses to other items.

No Minimum Time

No minimum period of time is required for trend data, although three years is recommended. Time periods might span five years or more for some results. Trends might be much shorter for some of the organization's improvement activities. Because of the importance of showing deployment and focus, new data should be included even if trends and comparisons are not yet well established.

**Compact
Presentation**

Presenting many results can be done compactly by using graphs and tables. Label graphs and tables for easy interpretation. Results over time or compared with others should be normalized—presented in a way (such as use of ratios) that takes into account various size factors. For example, if the organization's work force has been growing, reporting safety results in terms of accidents per 100 employees would permit more meaningful trend data that total accidents.

**Link Results
with Text**

Descriptions of results and the results themselves should be close together in the application. Use figure numbers that correspond to items. For example, the third figure for Item 6.1 would be 6.1-3. (See example below.)

The following graph illustrates data an applicant might present as part of a response to Item 6.1, Product and Service Quality Results. In the business overview and in Item 7.1, the applicant has indicated on-time delivery as a key customer requirement.

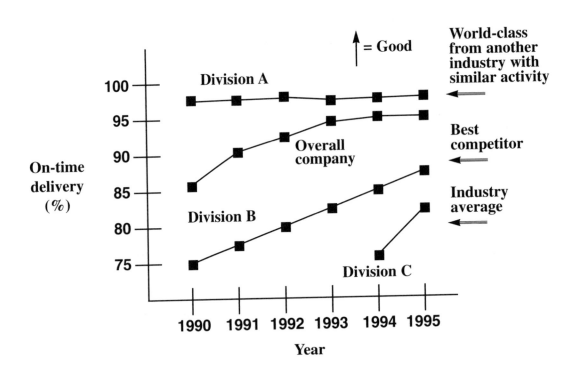

Figure 6.1-3.   On-time delivery performance.

Using the graph, the following characteristics of clear and effective data presentation are illustrated.

- A figure number is provided for reference to the graph in the text.
- Both axes and units of measure are clearly labeled.
- Trend lines report data for a key business requirement—on-time delivery.
- Results are presented for several years.
- Appropriate comparisons are clearly shown.
- The organization shows, using a single graph, that its three divisions separately track on-time delivery.
- An upward-pointing arrow appears on the graph indicating that increasing values are "good." Use a downward-pointing arrow to indicate that decreasing values are "good."

To help interpret the scoring guidelines, the following comments on the graphed results would be appropriate.

- The current overall organization performance level is excellent. This conclusion is supported by the comparison with competitors and with a world-class level.
- The organization exhibits an overall excellent improvement record.
- Division A is the current performance leader, showing sustained high performance and a slightly positive trend. Division B shows rapid improvement. Its current performance is near that of the best industry competitor, but trails the world-class level.
- Division C—a new division—shows rapid progress. Its current performance is not yet at the level of the best industry competitor.

Complete Data   Be sure results data are displayed for all relevant product and service characteristics, all relevant operational performance characteristics, and all relevant
supplier performance characteristics. If you identify relevant performance
measures and goals in other parts of the analysis (for example, Items 2.1,
2.3, 3.2, 5.1, 5.2, 5.3, and 5.4), be sure to include the results of these performance characteristics in Category 6.0. As each relevant performance measure
is identified in the assessment process, create a blank chart and label the
axes. As data are collected, populate the charts. If expected data are not provided in the application, examiners may assume the trends or levels are not
good. Missing data drive the score down just as poor trends do.

Break Out Data   Avoid aggregating the data. Where appropriate, break data into meaningful
components. If you serve several different customer groups, display performance and satisfaction data for each group. As the graph below demonstrates, one of the three trends is positive, although the average is positive.
Examiners will seek component data when aggregate data are reported.

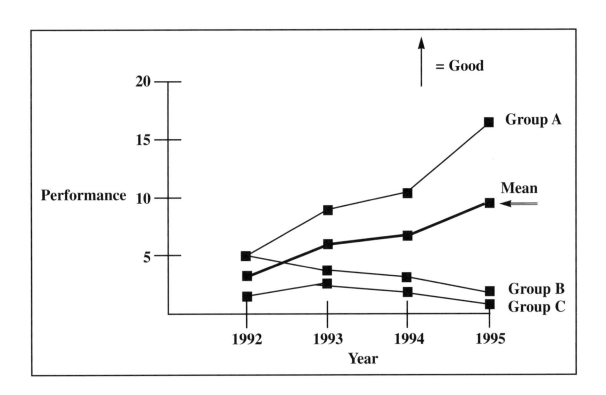

The Importance of Criteria Notes

Each item is followed by one or more notes that offer some insight and explanation about the item. Often, these notes suggest activities or measures that other organizations have used to meet the requirements of the item. There are many ways to manage a high performance system that are not included in the notes. Accordingly, notes should be considered suggestions and not requirements. However, most organizations would not go wrong by adopting the practices described in the notes.

Data and Measures

Comparison data are required for all items in Category 6.0 and Item 7.4. These data are designed to demonstrate how well the organization is performing. To judge performance excellence, one must possess comparison data. In the chart below, performance is represented by the line connecting the squares. Clearly, the organization is improving, but how "good" is it? Without comparison data, answering that question is difficult.

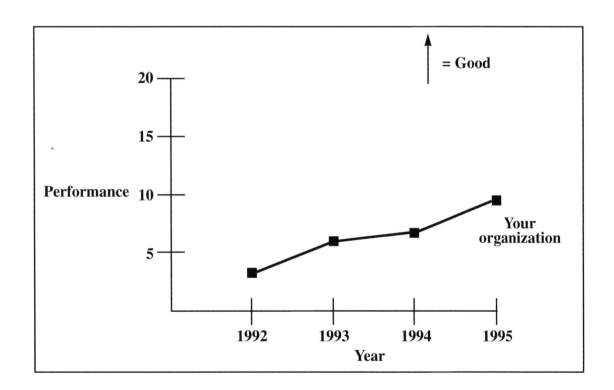

Now consider the chart with comparison data added.

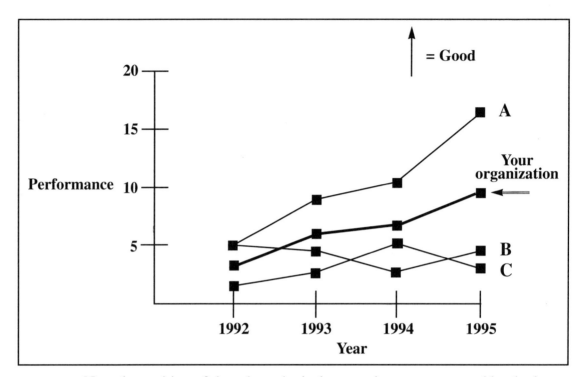

Note the position of three hypothetical comparisons, represented by the letters A, B, and C. Consider the following two scenarios.

- If **A** represents the industry average and both **B** and **C** represent area competitors, examiners would conclude the organization's performance was substandard, even though it is improving.

- If **A** represents a best-in-class (benchmark) organization and **B** represents the industry average, examiners would conclude that organizational performance is very good.

In both scenarios, the organizational performance remained the same but the examiner's perception of it changed.

Measures   Agreeing on relevant measures is a difficult task for organizations in the early phases of quality and performance improvement. The task is easier if the following guidelines are considered.

- Clearly define customer requirements. Clearly defined customer requirements require probing and suggesting, but they are easier to measure. For example, the customer of a new computer wants the equipment to be reliable. After probing to find what "reliable" means, we discover that the customer expects it to work all of the time. If it does stop working, the customer expects fast service: (1) prompt appearance at the site, (2) immediate access to parts, and (3) the ability to fix it right the first time.

- For each of the requirements above, identify a measure. For example, mean time between failures (MTBF) is one indicator of reliability but it does not account for all of the variation. Since the customer is concerned with run time, we must assess how long it took the repair technician to arrive at the site, diagnose the problem, and fix it. Measures include time in hours, days, weeks between failures, time in minutes between the service call and the computer regaining capability (time to fix), time in minutes waiting for parts, and the associated costs in terms of cash and worker effort.

- Collect and report data. Several charts would be required to display these factors.

Award Criteria Purposes

The Malcolm Baldrige National Quality Award criteria are the basis for making awards and for giving feedback to applicants. In addition, the criteria have three important roles in strengthening U.S. competitiveness.

- To help improve performance practices and capabilities
- To facilitate communication and sharing of best practices information among and within organizations of all types, based upon a common understanding of key performance requirements
- To serve as a working tool for managing performance, planning, training, and assessment

Award Criteria Goals

The criteria are designed to help companies enhance their competitiveness through focus on dual, results-oriented goals.

- Delivery of ever-improving value to customers, resulting in market-place success; and
- Improvement of overall organization performance and capabilities.

Core Values and Concepts

The award criteria are built upon a set of core values and concepts. These values and concepts are the foundation for integrating customer and organization performance requirements within a results-oriented framework. These core values and concepts follow.

Customer-Driven Quality

Quality is judged by customers. All product and service features and characteristics that contribute value to customers and lead to customer satisfaction and preference must be a key focus of an organization's management system. Value, satisfaction, and preference may be influenced by many factors throughout the customer's overall purchase, ownership, and service experiences. These factors include the organization's relationship with customers that helps build trust, confidence, and loyalty. This concept of quality includes not only the product and service characteristics that meet basic customer requirements, but also include those features and characteristics that enhance them and differentiate them from competing offerings. Such enhancement and differentiation may be based upon new offerings, combinations of product and service offerings, rapid response, or special relationships.

Customer-driven quality is thus a strategic concept. It is directed toward customer retention, market share gain, and growth. It demands constant sensitivity to emerging customer and market requirements, and measurement of the factors that drive customer satisfaction and retention. It also demands awareness of developments in technology and of competitors' offerings, and rapid and flexible response to customer and market requirements.

Success requires more than defect and error reduction, merely meeting specifications, and reducing complaints. Nevertheless, defect and error reduction and elimination of causes of dissatisfaction contribute significantly to the customers' view of quality and are thus also important parts of customer-driven quality. In addition, the organization's success in recovering from defects and errors ("making things right for the customer") is crucial to building customer relationships and to customer retention.

Leadership

An organization's senior leaders need to set directions and create a customer orientation, clear and visible values, and high expectations. Reinforcement of the values and expectations requires personal commitment and involvement. The leaders' basic values and commitment need to address all stakeholders and include areas of public responsibility and corporate citizenship. The leaders should guide the creation of strategies, systems, and methods for achieving excellence and building capabilities. The systems and methods in turn guide all activities and decisions of the organization. The senior leaders need to commit to the development of the entire work force and should encourage participation and creativity by all employees. Through their personal involvement in planning, communications, review of organization performance, and employee recognition, the senior leaders serve as role models, reinforcing the values and building leadership and initiative throughout the organization.

Continuous Improvement and Learning

Achieving the highest levels of performance requires a well-executed approach to continuous improvement. The term *continuous improvement* refers to both incremental and breakthrough improvement. Improvement needs to be embedded in the way the organization functions. Embedded means: (1) improvement is part of the daily work of all work units; (2)

improvement processes seek to eliminate problems at their source; and (3) improvement is driven by opportunities to do better, as well as by problems that must be corrected. Sources of improvement include employee ideas, research and development, customer input, and benchmarking or other comparative performance information.

Improvements may be of several types: (1) enhancing value to customers through new and improved products and services; (2) reducing errors, defects, and waste; (3) improving responsiveness and cycle time performance; (4) improving productivity and effectiveness in the use of all resources; and (5) improving the organization's performance in fulfilling its public responsibilities and serving as a corporate citizenship role model. Thus, improvement is intended not only to provide better products and services, but also to be more responsive and efficient—both conferring additional marketplace advantages. To meet these objectives, continuous improvement must contain cycles of planning, execution, and evaluation. This requires a basis—preferably a quantitative basis—for assessing progress and for deriving information for future improvement cycles. Such information should directly link performance goals and internal operations.

Employee Participation and Development

An organization's success in improving performance depends increasingly on the skills and motivation of its work force. Employee success depends increasingly on having opportunities to learn and to practice new skills. Companies need to invest in the development of the work force through education, training, and opportunities for continuous growth. Such opportunities might include classroom and on-the-job training, job rotation, and pay for demonstrated skills. Structured on-the-job training offers a cost-effective way to train and to better link training to work processes. Work force education and training programs may need to utilize advanced technologies, such as electronic support systems, computer-based learning, and satellite broadcasts. Increasingly, training, development, and work organizations need to be tailored to a diverse work force and to more flexible, high performance work practices.

Major challenges in the area of work force development include: (1) integration of human resource management—selection, performance, recognition, training, and career advancement; and (2) aligning human resource management with business plans and strategic change processes. Addressing these challenges requires acquisition and use of employee-related data on skills, satisfaction, motivation, safety, and well-being. Such data need to be tied to indicators of organization or unit performance, such as customer satisfaction, customer retention, and productivity. Through this approach, human resource management may be better integrated and aligned with business directions.

Fast Response

Success in competitive markets increasingly demands ever-shorter cycles for new or improved product and service introduction. Also, faster and more flexible response to customers is now a more critical requirement. Major improvement in response time often requires simplification of work organizations and work processes. To accomplish such improvement, the time performance of work processes should be among the key process measures. There are other important benefits derived from this focus: Response time improvements often drive simultaneous improvements in organization, quality, and productivity. Hence it is beneficial to consider response time, quality, and productivity objectives together.

Design Quality and Prevention

Business management should place strong emphasis on design quality—problem and waste prevention achieved through building quality into products and services and efficiency into production and delivery processes. In general, costs of preventing problems at the design stage are much lower than costs of correcting problems that occur "downstream." Design quality includes the creation of fault-tolerant (robust) or failure-resistant processes and products.

A major issue in competition is the design-to-introduction (product generation) cycle time. Meeting the demands of rapidly changing markets requires that companies carry out stage-to-stage coordination and integration (concurrent engineering) of functions and activities from basic research to commercialization. Increasingly, design quality also includes the ability to incorporate information gathered from diverse sources and databases, which combine factors such as customer preference, competitive offerings, marketplace changes, and external research findings and developments.

From the point of view of public responsibility, the design stage is a critical decision point. Design decisions affect process waste streams and the composition of municipal and industrial wastes. The growing demands for a cleaner environment mean that companies' design strategies need to include environmental factors.

Consistent with the theme of design quality and prevention, improvement needs to emphasize interventions "upstream"—at early stages in processes. This approach yields the maximum overall benefits of improvements and corrections. Such upstream intervention also needs to take into account the organization's suppliers.

Long-Range View of the Future

Pursuit of market leadership requires a strong future orientation and a willingness to make long-term commitments to all stakeholders—customers, employees, suppliers, stockholders, the public, and the community. Planning needs to anticipate many types of changes including those that may affect customers' expectations of products and services, technological developments, changing customer segments, evolving regulatory requirements, community/societal expectations, and thrusts by competitors. Plans, strategies, and resource allocations need to reflect these commitments and changes. A major part of the long-term commitment is developing employees and suppliers and fulfilling public responsibilities.

Management by Fact

Modern business management systems depend upon measurement, data, information, and analysis. Measurements must derive from the organization's strategy and encompass all key processes and the outputs and results of those processes. Facts and data needed for performance improvement and assessment are of many types, including: customer, product and service performance, operations, market, competitive comparisons, supplier, employee-related, and cost and financial. Analysis refers to extracting larger meaning from data to support evaluation and decision making at all levels within the organization. Such analysis may entail using data to reveal information—such as trends, projections, and cause and effect—that might not be evident without analysis. Facts, data, and analysis support a variety of organization purposes, such as planning, reviewing organization performance, improving operations, and comparing organization performance with competitors' or with best practices benchmarks.

A major consideration in the use of data and analysis to improve performance involves the creation and use of performance measures or indicators. Performance measures or indicators are measurable characteristics of products, services, processes, and operation that the organization uses to track and improve performance. The measures or indicators should be selected to best represent the factors that lead to improved customer, operational, and financial performance. A system of measures or indicators tied to customer and/or organization performance requirements represents a clear basis for aligning all activities with the organization's goals. Through the analysis of data from the tracking processes, the measures or indicators themselves may be evaluated and changed. For example, measures selected to track product and service quality may be judged by how well improvement in these measures correlates with improvement in customer satisfaction and customer retention.

Partnership Development

Companies should seek to build internal and external partnerships to better accomplish their overall goals.

Internal partnerships might include those that promote labor-management cooperation, such as agreements with unions. Agreements might entail employee development, cross-training, or new work organizations, such as high performance work teams. Internal partnerships might also involve creating network relationships among organization units to improve flexibility and responsiveness.

External partnerships might be with customers, suppliers, and education organizations for a variety of purposes, including education and training. An increasingly important kind of external partnership is the strategic partnership or alliance. Such partnerships might offer an organization entry into new markets or a basis for new products or services. A partnership might also permit the blending of an organization's core competencies or leadership capabilities with complementary strengths and capabilities or partners, thereby enhancing overall capability, including speed and flexibility. Internal and external partnerships should seek to develop longer-term objectives, thereby creating a basis for mutual investments. Partners should address the key requirements for success of the partnership, means of regular communication, approaches to evaluating progress, and means for adapting to changing conditions. In some cases, joint education and training could offer a cost-effective means to help ensure success.

Corporate Responsibility and Citizenship

An organization's management should stress corporate responsibility and encourage corporate citizenship. Corporate responsibility refers to basic expectations of the organization—business ethics and protection of public health, safety, and the environment. Health, safety, and environmental considerations include the organization's operations as well as the life cycles of products and services. Companies need to address factors such as resource conservation and waste reduction at their source. Planning related to public health, safety, and the environment should anticipate adverse impacts that may arise in facilities management, production, distribution, transportation, and use and disposal of products. Plans should seek to prevent problems, to provide a forthright organization response if problems occur, and to make available information needed to maintain public awareness, safety, and confidence. Inclusion of public responsibility areas within a performance system means meeting all local, state, and federal laws and regulatory requirements. It also means treating these and related requirements as areas for continuous improvement "beyond mere compliance." This requires that appropriate measures be created and used in managing performance.

Corporate citizenship refers to leadership and support—within limits of an organization's resources—of publicly important purposes, including areas of corporate responsibility. Such purposes might include education improvement, improving health care value, environmental excellence, resource conservation, community services, improving industry and business practices, and sharing of nonproprietary quality-related information. Leadership as a corporate citizen also entails influencing other organizations, private and public, to partner for these purposes. For example, individual companies could lead efforts to help define the obligations of their industry to its communities.

Results Orientation

An organization's performance system needs to focus on results. Results should be guided by and balanced by the interests of all stakeholders—customers, employees, stockholders, suppliers and partners, the public, and the community. To meet the sometimes conflicting and changing aims that balance implies, organization strategy needs to explicitly address all stakeholder requirements to ensure that actions and plans meet the differing needs and avoid adverse impact on any stakeholders. The use of a balanced composite of performance measures offers an effective means to communicate requirements, to monitor actual performance, and to marshal support for improving results.

Changes from the 1995 Award Criteria

Leadership

Item 1.2 now has two areas compared with three in 1995. Areas 1.2a and 1.2b from 1995 were combined, thus better integrating communications with other related organizational requirements. In addition, the organization performance review area (1.2b in 1996 and 1.2c in 1995) is now much more explicit in its requirements. The area now calls for nonfinancial and financial data related to the needs of all key stakeholders. It also calls for information on the tracking of progress relative to plans, competitive performance, and productivity in the use of assets.

Information and Analysis

Item 2.1 (Area 2.1a) now includes a requirement to provide information on the design of the organization's performance measurement system. This change is intended to enhance the diagnostic value of the item and strengthen the feedback to applicants.

Strategic Planning

Major planning concepts, most notably *key business drivers,* have been included in a Glossary of Key Terms.

High Performance Work

The meaning of *high performance work,* the focus of Item 4.2, has been included in the Glossary of Key Terms.

Human Resource Development and Management

An item has been created in Category 6.0 (Item 6.3) for reporting all human resource results.

Process Management

The meaning of *process* has been included in the Glossary of Key Terms.

Business Results

A new item, Human Resource Results (Item 6.3), has been created. This item is intended to provide a better focus on and a more comprehensive treatment of the human resource results required by the Human Resource Development and Management Category and previously included in the Company Operational and Financial Results (Item 6.2 in 1995).

Customer Focus and Satisfaction

Two items from 1995 (Customer Satisfaction Results and Customer Satisfaction Comparison) have been combined. The new item (Customer Satisfaction Results) integrates the requirements included in the two 1995 items.

Eligibility Categories and Restrictions

Basic Eligibility

Public Law 100-107 establishes the three eligibility categories of the award: Manufacturing, Service, and Small Business. Any for-profit business located in the United States or its territories may apply for the award. Eligibility for the award is intended to be as open as possible to all U.S. companies. Minor eligibility restrictions and conditions ensure fairness and consistency in definition. For example, publicly or privately owned, domestic or foreign-owned, joint ventures, incorporated firms, sole proprietorships, partnerships, and holding companies may apply. Not eligible are: local, state, and national government agencies; not-for-profit organizations; trade associations; and professional societies.

Award Eligibility Categories

Manufacturing

Companies or subunits of larger entities that produce and sell manufactured products or manufacturing processes, and producers of agricultural, mining, or construction products.

Service

Companies or subunits that sell services.

Small Business

Complete businesses with not more than 500 full-time employees. Business activities may include manufacturing and/or service. A small business must be able to document that it functions independently of any other businesses that are equity owners. If there are equity owners with some management control, at least 50 percent of the customer base of the small business' must be other than the equity owners.

Subunits

For purposes of the award, a subunit means a subsidiary, business unit, division, or like organization. In the Manufacturing and Service categories, subunits of a company might be eligible, but small businesses must apply as a whole. The following application conditions apply for subunits.

- The unit must be in existence for at least one year.
- The unit must have clear definition of organization as reflected in corporate literature, that is, the unit must function as a business entity.
- The unit must have more than 500 full-time employees, or the unit must have 25 percent of all company employees.
- The entire unit must be included in the application.

Restrictions on Eligibility

1. More than 50 percent of the applicant unit's employees must be located in the United States or its territories or more than 50 percent of the applicant unit's physical assets must be located in the United States or its territories.

2. At least 50 percent of a subunit's customer base must be free of direct financial and line organization control by the parent company.

3. Individual units or partial aggregations of units of "chain" organizations (a chain organization is an organization where each unit [subsidiary or franchise] performs a similar function or manufactures a similar product) are not eligible.

4. Company units performing any of the business support functions of the company are not eligible.

Multiple-Application Restrictions

1. A subunit and its parent company may not both apply for awards in the same year.

2. Only one subunit of a company may apply for an award in the same year in the same award category.

Future Eligibility Restrictions

1. If a company receives an award, the company and all its subunits are ineligible for a period of five years.

2. If a subunit receives an award, it is ineligible to apply for a period of five years.

3. If a subunit consisting of more than one-half of the total sales of a company receives an award, neither that company nor any of its other subunits are eligible to apply for a period of five years.

The Malcolm Baldrige National Quality Improvement

Act of 1987— Public Law 100-107

The Malcolm Baldrige National Quality Award was created by Public Law 100-107 and signed into law on August 20, 1987. The award program, responsive to the purposes of Public Law 100-107, led to the creation of a new public-private partnership. Principal support for the programs comes from the Foundation for the Malcolm Baldrige National Quality Award, established in 1988.

The award is named for Malcolm Baldrige, who served as Secretary of Commerce from 1981 until his tragic death in a rodeo accident in 1987. His managerial excellence contributed to long-term improvement in efficiency and effectiveness of government.

The Findings and Purposes Section of Public Law 100-107 states that:

1. the leadership of the United States in product and process quality has been challenged strongly (and sometimes successfully) by foreign competition, and our Nation's productivity growth has improved less than our competitors' over the last two decades.

2. American business and industry are beginning to understand that poor quality costs companies as much as 20 percent of sales revenues nationally and that improved quality of goods and services goes hand in hand with improved productivity, lower costs, and increased profitability.

3. strategic planning for quality and quality improvement programs, through a commitment to excellence in manufacturing and services, are becoming more and more essential to the well-being of our Nation's economy and our ability to compete effectively in the global marketplace.

4. improved management understanding of the factory floor, worker involvement in quality, and greater emphasis on statistical process control can lead to dramatic improvements in the cost of quality of manufactured products.

5. the concept of quality improvement is directly applicable to small companies as well as large, to service industries as well as manufacturing, and to the public sector as well as private enterprise.

6. in order to be successful, quality improvement programs must be management-led and customer-oriented, and this may require fundamental changes in the way companies and agencies do business.

7. several major industrial nations have successfully coupled rigorous private-sector quality audits with national awards giving special recognition to those enterprises the audits identify as the very best; and

8. a national quality award program of this kind in the United States would help improve quality and productivity by:

    A. helping to stimulate American companies to improve quality and productivity for the pride of recognition while obtaining a competitive edge through increased profits;

    B. recognizing the achievements of those companies that improve the quality of their goods and services and providing an example to others;

    C. establishing guidelines and criteria that can be used by business, industrial, governmental, and other organizations in evaluating their own quality improvement efforts; and

    D. providing specific guidance for other American organizations that wish to learn how to manage for high quality by making available detailed information on how winning organizations were able to change their cultures and achieve eminence.

Glossary

Alignment

Alignment refers to unification of goals throughout the company and consistency of processes, actions, information, and decisions among company units in support of these goals.

Effective alignment requires common understanding of purposes and goals and use of complementary measures and information to enable planning, tracking, analysis, and improvement at three levels: the organization level; the key process level; and the work unit level.

Benchmarking

The part of an improvement process in which an organization compares its performance against that of other organizations, determines how those organizations achieved higher performance levels, and uses the information to improve its own performance. Although it is difficult to benchmark some processes directly in some businesses, many of the things one organization does are very similar to things that others do. For example, most organizations move information and tangible products, pay people, train them, appraise their performance, and more. A key to successful benchmarking is to identify the process elements of work and find others who are the best at that process.

Continuous Improvement

The ongoing improvement of products, programs, services, or processes by small increments or major breakthroughs.

Customer

An organization or person who receives or uses a product or service. The customer may be a member or part of another organization or the same organization, or an end user.

Cycle Time

Cycle time refers to responsiveness and completion time measures— the time required to fulfill commitments or to complete tasks. Cycle time and related terms are used in the criteria booklet to refer to all aspects of time performance.

Time measurements play a major role in the criteria because of the great importance of time performance to improving competitiveness. Other time-related terms in common use are: set-up time, lead time, change-over time, delivery time, and time to market.

Data

Numerical information used as a basis for reasoning, discussion, determining status, decision making, and analysis.

Employee Involvement

A practice within an organization whereby employees regularly participate in making decisions on how their work is done, including making suggestions for improvement, planning, goal setting, and monitoring performance.

High Performance Work

High performance work refers to work approaches *systematically* directed toward achieving ever higher levels of overall performance, including quality and productivity.

Approaches to high performance work vary in form, function, and incentive systems. Effective approaches generally include: cooperation between management and the work force, including work force bargaining units; cooperation among work units, often involving teams; self-directed responsibility (sometimes called *empowerment*); individual and organizational skill building and learning; flexibility in job design and work assignments; an organizational structure with minimum layering (flattened), where decision making is decentralized and decisions are made closest to the front line; and regular use of performance measures, including comparisons. Some high performance work systems use monetary and nonmonetary incentives based upon factors such as organization performance, team and/or individual contributions, and skill building. Also, some high performance work approaches attempt to align the design of organizations, work, jobs, and incentives.

Indicator

When two or more measurements are required to provide a more complete picture of performance, the measurements are called *indicators.*

Integrated

Refers to the interconnections between the processes of a management system. For example, to satisfy customers an organization must understand their needs, convert those needs into designs, produce the product or service required, deliver it, assess ongoing satisfaction, and adjust the processes accordingly. People need to be trained or hired to do the work, and data must be collected to monitor progress. Performing only a part of the required activities is disjointed and not integrated.

Key Business Drivers

Key business drivers is a phrase used in the award criteria in connection with strategic planning and related goal setting. Key business drivers refer to principal company-level requirements, derived from short- and long-term strategic planning. Key business driver development represents the critical stage in planning when general strategies and goals are made sufficiently specific so that effective companywide understanding and ongoing action are possible. In simplest terms, key business drivers are those things the company must do well for its strategy to succeed.

An effective planning approach results in a clear basis (key business drivers)for consistent focus, communications, and deployment at three levels: the company level; the key process level; and the work unit level. Deployment of key business drivers requires analysis of overall resource needs and creation of aligned measures for all work units. Deployment might require specialized training for some employees or recruitment of personnel.

An example of a key business driver for a supplier in a highly competitive industry might be to develop and maintain a price leadership position. Deployment should entail design of efficient processes, analysis of resource and asset use, and creation of related measures of resource and asset productivity for all work units, aligned for the organization as a whole. It might also involve adoption of a cost-accounting system that provides meaningful activity-level cost information to support day-to-day work. Unit and/or team training should include priority setting based upon costs and benefits. Company-level analysis and review should emphasize overall productivity growth. Ongoing competitive analysis and planning should remain sensitive to technological and other changes that might greatly reduce operating costs for the organization or its competitors.

Leadership System

Leadership system refers to how leadership is exercised throughout the company—the way that key decisions are made, communicated, and carried out at all levels. It is based upon shared values, expectations, and purposes; communicated and reinforced via interactions among leaders and managers; reflected in the decisions the leaders make; and evident in the actions of the company. It includes the formal and informal bases and mechanisms for leadership development used to select leaders and managers, to develop their leadership skills, and to provide guidance and examples regarding behaviors and practices.

An effective leadership system creates clear values respecting the requirements of all stakeholders of the company and sets high expectations for performance and performance improvement. It builds loyalties and teamwork based upon the values and the pursuit of shared purposes. It encourages and supports initiative and risk taking, subordinates organization to purpose and function, and minimizes reliance on chains of command that require long decision paths. An effective leadership system includes mechanisms for the leaders' self-examination and improvement.

Measure

A direct measurement of performance. For example, the amount of time needed to receive an operational approval, the number of briefings given to customers, the number of program milestones achieved on schedule, or the time required to respond to a service call.

Measures and Indicators

Measures and indicators refer to numerical information that quantify (measure) input, output, and performance dimensions of processes, products, and services. Measures and indicators might be simple (derived from one measurement) or composite.

The award criteria do not make a distinction between measures and indicators. However, some users of these terms prefer the term *indicator:* (1) when the measurement relates entirely to performance and not to inputs; (2) when the measurement relates to performance but is not a direct or exclusive measure of such performance; for example, the number of complaints is an indicator of dissatisfaction, but not a direct or exclusive measure of it; and (3) when a performance or measure is a predictor (leading indicator) of some more significant performance, for example, gain in customer satisfaction might be a leading indicator of market share gain.

Performance

Performance refers to numerical results information obtained from processes, products, and services that permit evaluation and comparison relative to goals, standards, past results, and to others. Most commonly, the results address quality, efficiency, and time, and might be expressed in nonfinancial and financial terms.

Four types of performance are addressed in this criteria book: (1) operational; (2) product and service quality; (3) customer-related; and (4) financial.

Operational performance refers to performance relative to effectiveness and efficiency measures and indicators. Examples include cycle time, productivity, and waste reduction. Operational performance might be measured at the work unit level, the key process level, and the organization level.

Product and service quality performance refers to performance relative to measures and indicators of product and service requirements, derived from customer preference information. Examples include reliability, on-time delivery, defect levels, and service response time. Product and service quality performance generally relates to the organization as a whole.

Customer-related performance refers to performance relative to measures and indicators of customers' perceptions, reactions, and behaviors. Examples include customer retention, complaints, customer survey results, and market share. Customer-related performance generally relates to the organization as a whole.

Financial performance refers to performance using measures of cost and revenue, including asset utilization and asset growth. Financial measures are generally tracked throughout the organization and also are aggregated to give company-level, composite measures of performance. Examples include returns on investments, returns on assets, working capital productivity, and total factor productivity.

Process

Process refers to linked activities with the purpose of producing a product or service for a customer (user) within or outside the company. Generally, processes involve combinations of people, machines, tools, techniques, and materials in a systematic series of steps or actions.

In some situations, process performance might require adherence to a specific sequence of steps with documentation (sometimes formal) of procedures and requirements, including well-defined measurement and control steps.

In many service situations, particularly when customers are directly involved in one or more steps of the service, *process* is used in a more general way—to spell out what must be done, possibly including a preferred or expected sequence. If a sequence is critical, the service needs to include information for customers to help them understand and adhere to the sequence. Service processes involving customers require guidance to the servers on handling contingencies related to differing circumstances and to customers' actions or behaviors.

In cases such as strategic planning, research, and analysis, process does not necessarily imply formal sequences of steps. Rather, process implies general understandings regarding competent performance such as timing, options to be included, evaluation, and reporting. Sequences might arise as part of these understandings.

Prevention-Based

Seeking the root cause of a problem and preventing its recurrence rather than merely solving the problem and waiting for it to happen again (reactive posture).

Productivity

Productivity refers to measures of efficiency of the use of resources. Although the term is often applied to single factors such as labor, machines, materials, energy, and capital, the productivity concept applies as well to the total resources consumed in producing outputs. Overall productivity—usually called *total factor productivity*—is determined by combining the productivities of the different resources used for an output. The combination usually requires taking a weighted average of the different single factor productivity measures, where the weights typically reflect costs of the resources. The use of an aggregate measure such as total factor productivity allows a determination of whether or not the net effect of overall changes in a process—possibly involving resource tradeoffs—is beneficial.

Effective approaches to performance management require understanding and measuring single factor and total factor productivity, particularly in complex cases when there are a variety of costs and potential benefits.

Refinement

The result of a systematic process to analyze performance or a system and improve it.

Root Cause

The original cause or reason for a condition. The root cause of a condition is that cause which, if eliminated, guarantees that the condition will not recur.

Service Standard

A set, measurable level of performance. For example, an objective of an organization might be "prompt customer service." A service standard stipulates how prompt the service will be: "Equipment will be repaired within 24 hours," or "The phone will be answered by a person on or before the second ring."

System

A set of well-defined and well-designed processes for meeting the organization's quality and performance requirements.

Systematic Approach

A process that is repeatable and predictable, rather than anecdotal and episodic.

Values

The principles and beliefs that guide an organization and its people toward the accomplishment of its mission and vision.

Index

Comments and Areas for Improvement

Please give me your comments, feedback, and suggestions for making this book more useful. I believe in the importance of continuous improvement and in meeting your requirements. Your comments will help determine what improvements are made in the next edition.

	1 Needs Work	2	3 Satisfactory	4	5 Excellent
Structure and logic					
Flow diagrams					
Linkages					
Sample effective practices					
Met my overall expectations					

I read the book because:

The best part of the book was:

The least satisfactory part of the book was:

I would like the book to include:

General comments:

Name and contact information (optional):